EL MOUATAMID BEN ROCHD

History

of

Linguistics

To Haddadi and Touzani

Contents

Forward   5

1. Why study language?   8
2. History of linguistic studies   19
3. Language   22
4. Japan   27
5. China   32
6. Babylon   38
7. Panini   40
8. Aristotle   44
9. Arabs   53
10. Hebrews   70
11. Historicism   76
12. Saussure   88
13. Copenhagen   95
14. Prague   102
15. Marrism   133
16. Wittgenstein   136
17. Bloomfieldians   146

18. Chomsky   159

19. Phonology 176

20. Labov   180

21. Translation 186

22. Phonetics   193

Conclusion   199

Glossary   206

Bibliography   220

FORWARD

Swiss Ferdinand de Saussure (1916) is known as 'the father of modern Linguistics.' For others the 'champion of Linguistics' came later on in the person of American Noam Chomsky (1957). As a matter of fact, the infatuation for language, goes far earlier in the past, and was indeed felt under different horizons, in the Far and Middle East before reaching Europe and North America. This book is an attempt to give a glimpse on this long journey of language studies from remote areas of the world such as India (Panini), Iraq (Sibawaihi), Cordoba (Ibn Janah) and ancient Greece (Aristotle).

To put it in the most simple fashion, one can define 'LANGUAGE' as a 'coin' with two faces: 'sound and sense'. More sophisticated definitions were given by famous specialists. Their definitions remain dualist though: 'qawl/kalam' (Ibn Jinni), 'langue/parole' (Saussure), 'Deep/surface' (Chomsky), 'Classical/colloquial' (Ferguson) etc. 'Language' remains a puzzle to the best and a miracle for some

(Einstein?). Many were brought to the 'Labor' including philosophers (Spinoza), historians (Ibn Khaldun), psychologists (Watson), sociologists (Durkheim), and even brilliant amateurs (Jonathan Miller).

The student of linguistics soon finds options and ramifications that he has to favour one at the expense of the others. The major roads of the split are: micro-linguistics (phonetics, phonology, morphology, syntax, semantics, and pragmatics.) and macro-linguistics (sociolinguistics, psycholinguistics, computational linguistics, mathematical linguistics, historical linguistics, etc.)

'Historical linguistics' and 'history of linguistics' sound close. As a matter of fact, they are not, but are related in an inclusive relationship. History of linguistics must include a survey of historical Linguistics as one of its chapters. It was the 'fashion' of 19th c. European linguistic researchers (Schleicher and Paul). And then the student of linguistics must move to consider preceding trends and those that came later. Europe and America have largely dominated this field. Still, for a much broader perspective of our discipline, one must also include Arab linguists such as Sibawaihi, and Ibn Jinni, Hebrew linguists and philosophers such as Ibn Janah and Spinoza, besides the purely linguistic 'tenors'.

1. WHY STUDY LANGUAGE?

'Why study language?' you may ask. To answer this question, READ:

Dr. Mazen Al-Waer, "When someone introduces himself in a party as a doctor, people will wonder in which hospital he works, and when somebody introduces himself as a lawyer, everybody will think when he has a legal problem, the lawyer would be able to help. But when you introduce yourself as a linguist people will be astonished and ask what do you mean by linguistics? And when you try to explain to them that linguistics is a scientific study of languages, they will say, 'well, why do you bother and study languages since we speak them naturally? Do you think that linguistics can change people's opinions one day, and do you think the study of linguistics is important?"

Chomsky: "In our own intellectual tradition going back to the Greeks it has always been assumed, and I think correctly, that the most important topic to study is the human being, the question what is the nature of humans, and in particular, how the human mind works. There can hardly be a more significant topic for investigation for us than the human mind and how it functions. The most interesting aspects of the human mind are those intellectual achievements that are carried out naturally, that seem so obvious to us that we cannot even see at first that there is a problem to be studied. The first difficulty that you have to overcome if you want to study human beings is to try to attain a sense of wonder and surprise at the fact that you are able to do what you are able to do normally. If you do not think about it, it seems obvious that you just talk and say what is on your mind. But the question is: how are you able to do this? What is it about *the child* [italics mine] that makes it possible for the child to acquire this ability but does not make it possible for *an ape or a dog* [italics mine] or any other organism to acquire this ability? What is this capacity? What underlies it? What are its properties? What are its features?

The psychologist, Wolfgang Kohler, once remarked that it is necessary to develop a kind of *"psychic distance"* [italics mine] from the acts that you perform naturally. You have to be able to look at them as it were from the outside, to recognize how amazing they are, before you can begin to try to find out what are the capacities on which these acts are based. It is not a problem when you study, say, physics because, since we are studying something that is external to us, we already have psychic distance. We do not move the planets so therefore the fact that the planets move already seems remarkable. But since we are the ones who are doing the speaking, what we are doing sometimes does not seem remarkable, but rather somewhat obvious. However, it is really much more remarkable than the fact that the planets are moving the way they are."

(Dr. Mazen Al-Waer, 1980).

PHILOSOPHY

The ultimate goal of philosophers has always been the pursuit of TRUTH. But usually, they (and people in general) disagree about what is true and what is false [cf. Shakespeare's "wisdom and goodness"]. In Europe alone, there were indeed big and bitter intellectual fights, in the Middle Ages, about the sources of (true) knowledge to begin with. Some believed it should be ecclesiastic (Church), others opted for rational (reason), still others for empiricist (sense data) sources. The Pope in Rome, Martin Luther and Hegel represent the first trend. French René Descartes (*Discours de la méthode*) represents the second [cf. Deists]. English Roger Bacon is considered to be the pioneer of the last one (followed by Francis Bacon's *Novum Organum*).

There are, at least, three levels of influence of philosophy on linguistics, viz. 'ideological umbrella', epistemology and (more specifically) linguistic theory. The first one – ideology [cf. Marr] or religion [cf. Pike] – concerns the linguist as much as the layman in a given society. It is a sort of general umbrella that covers all members of a given society. Epistemology [theory of knowledge] concerns the scientist – whatever his specialty may be; as each researcher is busy digging his own (narrow) field not knowing how to situate himself vis-à-vis other scientists. Epistemology will guide him find his position and his relation with researchers in neighboring disciplines.

The last level of influence of philosophy is found in linguistic theorizing. After observation and experiments, the linguist, like all other scientists, opts for the construction of general theories – using reason and logic. He is actually philosophizing (hence, the appellation "PhD" as the top title for every discipline).

PSYCHOLOGY

Many people believe that the structure of language and its general features are universal and are deeply embedded in the human mind. At any rate the human body displays an amazing organic unity synchronized and harmonized by God. Without signals from the nervous system no air would escape from the throat to produce speech sounds. So no separation is possible between speech, biology and physiology; nor is it possible to separate them from the ideas which are shaped by speaking.

Language is closely linked to psychology. In the 19th and early 20th centuries, language had soon attracted the attention of American psychologists such as Watson and Skinner (see Glossary), amongst others. They were the representatives of the Bahaviourist School of psychology in the US in the 50s. They were themselves influenced by the works of

Russian biologist Pavlov [see glossary]. The latter is the initiator of 'stimulus-response' brain mechanisms, using dogs for his experiments.

By opposition to this school, Chomsky's innate theory suggests that *the human child is unique* as he comes to life pre-programmed for language acquisition. Chomsky seems to have in some sort revived Plato's notion of 'prenatal life'.

SCIENCE

Linguistics is usually defined as 'the science of languages'. We may then wonder about science itself; its foundations, stages, limits, etc. and how it could apply to languages? The human language is essentially made up of sounds and words organized in a structure and conveying meaning.

Linguistics is a science, like physics or biology, because it follows the scientific stages which are: *observation, hypothesis, experiment* (not to confuse with experience i.e. experiences that one has in his own life, happy, cheerful, etc.) and finally *theory*. Linguistics, as Chomsky noted, is a special science, since language is part of our person. So we tend to take it for granted. We do not even see that there is a problem to be studied unlike when we study, for instance, the motion of the stars. So what we need to do first is to try and achieve a certain *psychic-distance* [see above] before we can start our inquiry i.e. a certain detachment; objectivity.

The English proverb rightly says 'familiarity breeds contempt' or 'familiarity breeds stupidity'. My hand has been with me and served me for years. I do not see anything amazing about it, as I should! Now, each one of the four scientific stages has its own defects and limitations. It is perhaps difficult for us to achieve psychic-distance when studying language because Arabic is our language, French is the language of those who made our parents work like donkeys, English is full of figures and imperialism. So, you cannot really achieve 'psychic-distance' i.e. absolute objectivity.

The first scientific principle, i.e. observation has problems too; like visual illusions. We all know about the railway bars. You must have noticed that when you observe those long parallel bars, they seem to narrow progressively till they merge into one another. This is one of the problems with observation. Our senses cannot be trusted hundred per cent. Another example, we all think we know the color of blood – red, but once you look at it in the microscope, you find that it is yellow.

In linguistics, our observation is usually auditory. We hear sounds and utterances but again we face problems of perception. I remember once being told about the Scottish legend of the bird called *haggis* [who happens to have one leg shorter than the other to suit the leaning slopes of the hill!] I had problems determining whether it was with an 's' or a 't' viz. *haggis* or *haggit*.

After the problems of perception, we face problems with formulating scientific hypotheses. I suggested once to my students to explain the biological problem of two rotten pieces of meat, one containing maggots and one without. Some suggested that the origin of these maggots was the sun, others time, etc. They were all wrong, because the true answer was the flies. Some ninetieth century scientists had suggested that it was the meat itself that produced the maggots by *spontaneous generation*. So we can see that hypotheses are just a game of imagination. This is for those who may think that science is hundred per cent objective, concrete, tangible and true.

Hypothesis leads you to a series of experiments, which are again a mere game of *trial and error* tests. (cf. *bikussuf!*) Add to that the fact that you might be short-sighted, your hand may shake while measuring say the length of a table, your ruler may not be as *sharp* as it should be. So all these human and instrumental shortcomings give doubtful results. You could try and eliminate…Sorry, reduce those defects both in quantity and quality by improving your instruments and by repeating your experiments as many times as possible. Still, the result is quantitative and a mere approximation [cf. 'Delta d'Erreur'!]

As you cannot count the number of red blood globules of a human being, you work by induction. [See the story of that American tourist who said, 'Moroccans are crazy!' from a shop experience. He made a hasty 'scientific' generalization, instead of a solid LOGICAL deduction]. Scientific theories are further based on probabilities. When the Americans send their missiles [from Kennedy Canaveral Cape /keip/] to some planet, say **Mars**, they are never sure about where it will land or where it would come back with exactitude! All they can tell is **probabilities**. This is the opposite of how *assertive* (pseudo-scientific) *minds* tend to work. Finally, science is abstract e.g. a human mouth, for the phonetician, is no longer a real mouth made of bones, nerves and muscles. It is simply two curved lines. You can see how science is far from reality, but we accept it in the absence of better means. This is the lot of the mortals!

Another example: once upon a time in Europe, there were scientists who believed that they had discovered and known everything – especially doctors. They believed that there was nothing new they could see that they had not already seen. But there came a 'little' biologist who said, wait a minute! There are biological forms that cannot be seen to the mortals, yet they are responsible for the death of millions of them, each year. Who was that scientist? What did he discover? And how did he prove his claim? It was very simple (!), **Pasteur** (1828-1885) by accident!

Finally, 'theory': it is 'a formal set of ideas that is intended to explain why something happens or exists".(...) It's mere **philosophy**.

2. HISTORY OF LINGUISTIC STUDIES

For many scholars, the twentieth century was the starting point of serious (scientific) research in linguistics. It was mainly concentrated in Europe and North America. "After world war II, it appears that the histories by Malmberg (1964) and others fulfilled a similar function of summing up previous attainments in linguistic science. This time the focus of attention was post-1916 period in the history of linguistics, following the success story of Saussure's *Cours*, with its perceived emphasis on a non-historical approach to language." (Koerner and Asher, 1995)

"In 1980, Frederick Newmeyer published a book which constitutes the best example to date of this pro-domo, *whiggish* type of history writing. It selected and reinterpreted past linguistic research in an attempt to prove his view that linguistics was made a science only in 1955 or in 1957, and by Chomsky, and that previous work was totally inadequate…(Newmeyer's *Linguistics in America* (1980) "(ibid)

Still, other (rather shy!) attempts to write about the history of linguistics, going beyond euro-centrism started to point out their heads. Amongst the best of these works, one can mention: Aren's *Sprachwischenshft* (1955), Robins, R.H. *A Short history of linguistics* (1967), Samson G. *Schools of Linguistic* (1980), *and* excellent Koerner and Asher's *Concise History of the Language Sciences* (1995).

So the 'fashion' was to ignore remote geographical origins of linguistics, the subject supposedly started in the twentieth century. By opposition to this narrow (ideological) denial of anything coming from outside Europe and North America, some suggested recognizing and benefiting from broader horizons. "The best known example is probably Leonard Bloomfield who stated in a number of his publications that he was making use of concepts and techniques that were to be found in Panini's work on Sanskrit produced some two and a half millennia ago." (ibid)

Bloomfield further described Panini's work, on other occasions, as a "monument of intelligence."

For much broader perspectives of our discipline, one must also include Arab linguists such as Sibawaihi, and Ibn Jinni, and Hebrew linguists and philosophers such as Ibn Janah and Spinoza.

3. LANGUAGE

Albert Einstein once said, " There are two ways to live your life. One is as though nothing is a miracle. The other is as though everything is a *miracle*." (Awakin Org.)

So, obviously LANGUAGE is a *miracle*, if not the miracle of miracles. It is the best thing that man was God-given. It is a so-wonderful miracle that is has attracted the attention of early philosophers such as Plato and Aristotle, to modern philosophers like Austin and Wittgenstein. They all tried to capture the nature of this 'miracle' by giving it acceptable –reasonable- definitions. Some have succeeded to some extent in their endeavour and some have only "lured the fly into the bottle!" Starting from the nineteenth century, language has become the field of research of the specialists, viz. philologists such as Hermann Paul and August Schleicher, and more recently –modern linguists: Saussure, Bloomfield and Noam Chomsky (in the Western tradition)!

The language miracle can be clearly seen, as it is the key to man's communication with his fellow men!! Man was given the secret and the power to give symbols to (referents), i.e. different places (Paris, NY), people (Jesus, Marx) and different things (tree, table) by naming them. Man assigns uttered-expressions to concrete objects. This has a tremendous value in his life. We can appreciate this only by imagining a world without language: the extreme difficulty to work, if we did not have this semiotic power; the hardship of communication and bitter interrelations when we would have to bring about the **thing** itself that we have to talk about in front of our very eyes, say a tree, or go to the Himalayas, or bring the person, we want to talk about (no backbiting!). This **situation** would have been a tremendous hardship making our lives close to impossible. (cf. Aboriginal Australians!)

LANGUAGE can be seen as a coin with two faces i.e. "sound and sense." This is to put it in the most simplistic way. The specialists have much more to say about this subject; its NATURE, ORIGIN and USE.

As a first approximation, we could say that Languages differ in many aspects (and look alike indeed in many others). So when you listen to a foreign language you get the impression that you are hearing a stretch of unintelligible sounds. If you read an alien language, it is as **"if you give a book to an illiterate soldier, he will take it up-side-down, and all he will see is barbed wire."** (Professor Khalid Touzani)(!)

For the native speaker though, each stretch of sound switches in an image in his mind. The word "Paris" for instance stands for the Eiffel tower, even to the remote Gujarati, Igbo or Hausa speaker. Still, there is a difference between 'know how to drive a car' and how 'its mechanics works' when you first ignite the engine. The nature of each phenomenon remains to be defined – language in this case.

Many have been interested in this "phenomenon-miracle" including religious people, philosophers, sociologists, psychologists, philologists and finally modern linguists.

WHAT IS LANGUAGE?

This question, raises many others:

A) What's the use of linguistics?

B) How dialects develop and change;

C) Ideas about whether (and how) our language affects the way we think;

D) How children learn to speak;

E) How all the parts of language fit together;

F) To find the parts of our brain which hold different grammatical items, exotic languages, with complicated, sentence and word structures;

G) How language evolved;

H) The spell-checker on our PC (see "grammarly" for instance);

I) Synthetic speech on your telephone, including convincing intonation;

J) Monolingual and bilingual dictionaries;

K) Automatic translation systems;

L) Teaching Methods and learning foreign languages;

M) Later life and speech problems.

N) Linguistics relations with neighbouring disciplines: psychology, philosophy, epistemology, etc.

4. JAPAN

Although Japan is proud of its multi-facets culture, in linguistics, it unfortunately, lacks a linguist of the stature of Indian PANINI. The external influences in this domain were many: Indian, Chinese and Western, especially German philological influences of the nineteenth century (see Schleicher et al.)

The first typically Japanese effort was due to the relatively recent *kokugaku* (national education). The early introduction of the Chinese writing system (KANJI) and the introduction of Buddhism to Japan provided a certain stimuli. Many groups of scholars appeared including Japanese and non-Japanese philologists, especially the *Kokugaku* school that advocated the return to ancient Japanese values.

Japanese had no writing system, so it borrowed Chinese *Kanji* system (ideogram?), as early as the fourth century AD. To deal with Japanese complex inflectional morphology a second system was used; the *Kana* system. It is a phonetic system based on syllabic structure, and considered as a simplified version of *Kanji*.

Japanese linguistic situation was somewhat a 'Diglossia'(?) or, at least based on two systems: it was the dichotomy of 'private' (native Japanese) versus official (Chinese) with honorific terms (Sensei!)

Early studies in Japan were carried by Buddhist monks at the Confucian academy of Kyoto. The study of Sanskrit led to much work in translation. Buddhist **Sutras** circulated freely amongst monks, who were usually sent to China to learn. So, Sanskrit and Chinese dominated this period. *Zaitoki* is a record of the phonetic and phonological representations of these two languages. Phonetic terms equivalent of 'dental', 'nasal' and 'labial' were used to explain Sanskrit alphabet.

The Confucian academy was established around the 12th century, to educate future officials of Japan on the Chinese model. This double heritage led to the development of the famous '50-sounds chart':

50 SOUNDS CHART

A) a   ka ya sa ta na ra ha ma wa

B) i   ki i si ti ni ri hi mi wi

C) u   ku yu su tu nu ru hu mu u

D) e   ke e se te ne re he me we

E) o   ko yo so to no ro ho mo wo

"Chinese and Sanskrit influences are thought to account for the development of the so-called 50-sounds chart. This table is a phonological arrangement of the Japanese kana syllabary, listing syllables with the same vowel in horizontal rows and syllables with an identical or related Initial consonant in vertical columns." (Stefan Kaiser 1995)

Portuguese missionaries who arrived to Japan as early as the sixteenth century, sought to study the Japanese language as a first step in their missionary endeavor, producing a series of books, based on Latin grammar.

Moving further, "the (1778) Ayuisho is a work of great originality and deep insights into the workings of the Japanese language, amazingly free from influence from earlier research except for the work on Chinese particles by Fujitani's elder brother, the Confucian philosopher and Chinese grammarian Minagawa Kien, and possibly scholars of classical Chinese." Motoori Norinaga (1730-1801) influenced by earlier Kokugana scholars such as Keichu based his research on inductive empirical research.

MODERN PERIOD in Japanese linguistic scholarship can be traced back as early as the year 1886, with the establishment of the Tokyo Imperial University, western scholars such as B.H. Chamberlain and Humboldt were there to train Japanese students, including most brilliant Kasotoshi Ueda (1867-1937). The latter brought Paul Hermann's comparative approach from his studies in Germany.

By opposition to B.H. Humboldt who considered Chinese as lacking discrete speech categories, Suzuki's advocated (universal) word classes, for Chinese as well as for Japanese, in spite of the differences between the two languages. Chinese and Japanese stand poles apart in terms of characterization of word classes. One obvious viz. Japanese and one 'hidden' viz. Chinese.

British Chamberlain and Aston brought in their genetic approach, later developed by **Hattori** (1908-95). The work culminated in Yoshio Yamada's (1873-1958) grammar of Japanese in its own right. "Yamada can be placed in the tradition of early modern scholars such as Fujitanui Nariakira, whom he rated highly, but he reinterpreted and systematized their work in the light of the work of European linguists such as Sweet and Heyse, and the experimental psychologist Wundt." (Stefan Kaiser (1995:45)

5. CHINA

According to William S. Y. Wang and R.E. Asher (1995): "Of all the living languages of the world, Chinese has the longest unbroken recorded history, with texts in the language dating from as long ago as 35 centuries." According to Gleason (1969): "the most extensive language family in eastern Asia is the Sino-Tibetan", and therefore difficult to analyse from a European perspective.

"The cause of the differences can be seen to lie largely in the typology of the languages involved...Chinese grammar made little use of inflectional morphology. In addition, while the writing systems of India and Europe are essentially alphabetic, Chinese is written with morph-syllabic graphs."

METALINGUISTIC SPECULATION

"The earliest known linguist thinker of major importance is the philosopher Xun Zi, the date of whose birth is variously estimated as falling at different points within the period 335-313 BC. His best known work is Zheng Ming 'the rectification of names'), which goes back to a group of several sentences in the analects of Confucius." According to him "words have no intrinsic content or correctness...when the convention is established and the custom formed, the words then have content."

LEXICOGRAPHY

"Hsu Shen first century produced Shuo Wen Jie Zi (Explanations of Simple Characters And Analysis of Complex Characters) this pioneering work remains one of the most important in the history of Chinese lexicography... it deals with 9.353 characters." "to order them in accordance with a system of 540 radicals. Because of the correspondence between meaning and shape of the radicals...it codifies the Liu Shu, or the 6 principles"

"It is the fact that alphabets in their use relate closely, if not always entirely systematically, to the sequence of phonological segments in the language for which they are used." The language face-to-face dichotomy is referred to as "Hsu Shen's xing // sheng" i.e shape and sound.

DIALECTIC GEOGRAPHY

Yang Xiong's (53 BC -18 AD) work represents "the earliest extant work of this sort (geographical variation of language)." The data he gathered in so-called 'field trips' to different regions of China was in fact carried out in Chungan, the Han capital, where he asked soldiers and officials coming from different parts of **China** and being on duty in the capital. This is similar to the Moroccan dialects, i.e West vs. East dialectal variation e.g. /Xizzu daba vs. zrudija Druk/ "Carrots NOW!"

This double dimension of language variation concerns historical as well as geographical differences. His dichotomy Fang yan means 'region' and 'speech' respectively. This distinction has more to do with sociolinguistic data i.e. different words denoting different entities according to the different regions. This is used in modern times in the sense of 'dialect.' Given the wide extent of the Han Empire of the time.

PHONOLOGICAL STUDIES

"In 1978 the discovery of a set of 65 bronze bells lips which were cast 2.500 years ago. These bells can be struck at two different points to produce two distinct musical tones. Clear evidence for the claim relating to speech production is to be found in the second-century BC Ling Shu Juing, a work of anatomy which contains an account of the function of the various organs of speech, including the epiglottis, the uvula, the tongue, and the lips."

There are two formulas concerning for the pronunciation of a character: "that is to say that character X is said to be read as charcter Y (...) that is to say that a formula for *du ruo* would be of the type X=Y, whereas *xing sheng* could be satisfactorily represented by X = s+p, the formula indicating that the character has the *signific* of s and the *phonetic* of p, the components that make up X."

"With the spread of Buddhism to China came knowledge of some of the ancient Sanskrit sutras...so the need to translate and transliterate the Sanskrit sutras led to the development in china of new ideas.

"An early historical Phonologist was (...) some 4 centuries ago, Chen Di (1540-1620), who was fully aware of the fact that languages change over time, he attempted to reconstruct the pronunciation of the poems by different poets compiled in 6th c BC. The outcome of which was an anthology of 305 poems by unknown poets. The poems themselves cover a period of perhaps as much as 500 years but share a common pattern of rhyming."

TWENTIETH CENTURY DEVELOPMENTS

"During the twentieth century, the Chinese linguistic tradition has largely merged into international community of linguistic scholarship."

" while attempts to apply models based on European languages to the study of Chinese grammar led to obvious failure during the early 1900, efforts to investigate Chinese syntax using more sophisticated theories developed in the west promise more useful results. At the same time, such efforts have a reciprocal effect of extending as well as refining and enriching such theories by confronting them with typological features found chiefly in the languages of China typology "one example of such enrichment is the incorporation into theories of phonological of the features and methods which are necessary for the analysis of tones." (Wang, 1967).

1991 saw the creation of International Association of Chinese Linguistics.

6. BABYLON

The Babylonian linguistic tradition is considered by many scholars as the 1st grammatical tradition ever (even before ancient Egypt?) (see the Holy Bible). Its literary Texts are dated more than 2000 years before Christ. It consists of cuneiforms diagrams.

CUNEIFORM IDEOGRAMS (??)

The discovered ancient Sumerian tablets, were supposedly used for administrative purposes to begin with. That is to say to record the lists of workers (slaves?), their duties and the intersection between the two well-established lists. The lists were monthly and yearly based. They included inventories, rations, receipts and *rosters*. [People's lists!]

From the purely linguistic perspective, this gave rise to most crucial and important school known as the *Scribal School* of ancient Mesopotamia, the primary role of which was the transmission of administrative work. It soon shifted to a transmission of the writing system and therefore, the first linguistic glimpses, transforming ideograms into a phonological system i.e. from **Logographic** (??) to phonological syllabic system. It all started with signs representing animals and different daily artefacts to ultimately a Sumerian lexicon (words). It was an attempt to put the 'world into words' as Professor Patrick Griffiths would put it. The signs of Sumerian were more or less adequate representations of the notions of astronomy, medicine and religious beliefs, amongst other human needs.

The listing of the words led logically and naturally to the entry of grammatical notions, especially with the shift from Sumerian language to Akkadian (see Landsberger et al. 1956 *Marerialien Zum Sumerischen Lexikon*).

The translation of parallel lists of the two languages saw the emerging of a special genre of texts which gave Akkadian equivalents to Sumerian signs to obtain a range of systematically different forms of the same word. Most of which were pronouns, demonstratives, and especially verbs; "different detailed solutions were adopted for different verbs, although certain features of organization remain constant throughout the texts. The following is an outline of the solution adopted in the largest verbal paradigm (...) which deals with the verb: "du/nen" Sumerian = "alaku" Akkadian "go":

	SUMERIAN	AKKADIAN	
A)	nen-na	alik	'go!'
B)	ga-nen	lullik	'may I go?'
C)	he-nen	lillik	'may he go?'
D)	an-du	illak	'he goes'

The Sumerian language belongs to the Semitic language family. As such, like most ancient Semitic languages, it has a well-known and an important literature. Akkadian (Babylonian) and Sumerian, which are of unknown relationship are the chief languages of the vast cuneiform literature from Mesopotamia. (Gleason 1969)

In this respect, the Sumerian *Scribal School* can be considered as the oldest school of linguistics ever. Also, the cuneiform writing system developed by the Sumerians in Mesopotamia is considered as the 'mother' of all subsequent alphabets of the world.

7. PANINI

"The Indian tradition was the most ancient period as far as the study of language is concerned. The great Indian figure in this domain at that time was Panini (4th BC), whose work had a great deal of influence on the scholarship in India and abroad, even nowadays. Panini is an ancient Indian grammarian (520-460 BC) who lived in Grandhara and is most famous for his grammar of Sanskrit.

In India, people believed in successive incarnations and had a sacred book called the Vedas. Some non-native speakers of Sanskrit used to read the Vedas incorrectly. So Panini wrote the Astadhyayi (his 8 books) in order to set rules for that language. He is known particularly for his formulation of the 3.959 rules of Sanskrit morphology in his Book. Panini's grammar is highly systematised and technical. The Inherent units of his analytic approach are concepts of the phoneme, the morpheme and the root, which were only recognized by western linguists some two millennium later.

It is not known whether Panini himself used writing for the composition of his work. Some people argue that a work of such complexity would have been impossible to compile without written notes, while others allow for the possibility that he might have composed it with the help of a group of students whose memories served him as 'notepads'. Writing first appears in India in the form of the Brahmin script from around the sixth century BC, so it is also possible that he would have known and used a writing system."

Leonard Bloomfield recognized, on many occasions, his debt to Panini's linguistic insights. He described Panini's work as a "monument of intelligence."

8. ARISTOTLE

The Greeks and the Romans fought for hegemony for centuries. Then something strange happened: the victor and the defeated became one. The Romans defeated the Greeks militarily (148 BC), and the Greeks defeated the Romans culturally. The outcome of the battle was the union; known as the Greco-Roman civilization.

GRECO-ROMANS

"These schools go back to the Greek philosophers who considered that grammar was a branch of philosophy. They were concerned with the written language, as grammar in the Greek time meant "the art of writing". Greek philosophers discovered many things that had to do with language."

PLATO (429-347 BC)

"Plato discovered parts of speech or syntactic categories of the Greek language. He distinguished between nouns and verbs on logical grounds. For him, verbs express actions, whereas nouns are descriptive representations of the names of actions and their doers."

DONATUS (4th AD)

"In ancient Rome, there was a serious study of Latin as it is the "original language of the *New Testament*. The most influential Roman grammarian of the fourth century was Donatus, who wrote two grammars: *Ars Minor* and *Ars Major*. The first deals with word classes whereas the second book deals with morphology, syntax and a prescriptive grammar of Latin."

ARISTOTLE FORMAL LOGIC

Aristotle (384-322 BC) was the tutor of Alexander the Great. He was born in Macedonia. Together with Plato, he is considered as one of the greatest philosophers that the world has ever known. He was a true scholar and academic with an interest in several intellectual disciplines ranging from astronomy and rhetoric to politics and philosophy. His major was certainly logic. Aristotelian logic, also known as *Formal Logic* is based on PROPOSITION, SYLLOGISM and CONTRADICTION. He set the rules of formal logic in his notorious book *The Organon*.

1. TRUTH

Truth has been the main concern of logicians, philosophers and semioticians, in the past and the present. They divide truth into analytic (deductive) and synthetic (observational). In the absence of the latter they use the former. In the beginning, there is the word. Each word is connected to concepts, and then comes syntax into play. The combination of two words or more opens the door for truth. It is technically known as sentence or proposition. A proposition can be either true (T) or false (F). Each discourse consists of premises and a conclusion (**proposition**). If the premises are true, the conclusion is true and if the premises are false, the conclusion is false. Meaning can also shift from denotation which is (original sense) to connotation which is open-ended, e.g. *popular, freedom, democracy*, etc.

Proposition consists of a subject followed by a predicate. The subject is usually an entity; e.g. a person, an object:

The teacher is here

The chair is here

The predicate is an attribute of the subject. According to Aristotle, the number of predicates is 10, referred to as the Ten Categories:

2. THE TEN CATEGORIES

Substance (man, horse)

Quantity (two cm long)

Quality (white, grammatical)

Relation (double, half, greater)

Place (in the lyceum)

Time (last year)

Position (lies, sits)

State (has shoes)

Action (cuts, burns)

Affection (is cut, is burnt)

PROPOSITION

We will be mainly concerned with analytic truth value of propositions. The truth value of each proposition is fixed by a binary system consisting of either a tautology (T) or a contradiction (F). Consider the following proposition:

It is cold and windy

This proposition can be analyzed as consisting of two logically equivalent propositions:

It is cold, and

It is windy.

The first one can be either true or false. If we posit that it is true, then its negation must be false and vice versa: if we posit that it is false then its negation must be true. Call it P and its negation –P; we can obtain the following truth-table:

P	-P
T	F
F	T

The friend of my friend is my friend,

The enemy of my friend is my enemy

The friend of my enemy is my enemy

The enemy of my enemy is my friend!

Considering the compound proposition (conjunction): 'it is cold and windy' that we have analyzed as consisting of two propositions; call them P and Q; its truth-table will be as follows:

P	Q	P&Q
T	T	T
T	F	F
F	T	F
F	F	F

(Ben Rochd. 1994. *Generative Grammar*. Ms, UW)

CONTRADICTION

A contradiction is the combination of two propositions sharing the same subject and the same categories; except that one is affirmative and the other is negative. The truth value of a contradiction is always false (F).

P	-P	P&-P
T	F	F
F	T	F

Dialectics is based on contradiction.

SYLLOGISM

A syllogism consists of a major premise, a minor premise and a conclusion, e.g.

All men must die (MAJOR PREMISE)

Socrates is a man (MINOR PREMISE)

Socrates must die (CONCLUSION)

To reach the conclusion, you play down the middle term, in our case men/man (i.e. the subject of the major premise and the predicate of the minor premise) and you join the subject of the minor premise with the predicate of the major premise.

Moving to metaphysical considerations, Aristotle again used syllogism to state: "since motion must always exist and must not cease, there must necessarily be something, either one thing or many, that first initiated motion, and this first mover must be unmoved –the unmoved mover: GOD [THEOS]"

CONDITIONALS

A conditional proposition is a compound of two propositions; the truth of one depends on the truth of the other (disjunction vs. implication). It is a stipulation, or provision, that needs to be satisfied. Something that must exist or be the case or happen in order for something else to do so; as in 'the will to live is a condition for survival'.

A conditional proposition is a sentence/proposition of the form 'If A then B':

A disjunction is true if one part is true and the other false:

You are either a Moroccan or a non-Moroccan.

You are either Moroccan or French.

A conditional proposition (implication) is true if both parts are true and false if both parts are false as in:

If I had money I would be happy.

Conditionals are either hypothetical or categorical.

(Ben Rochd, 2006. *Ideas*)

9. ARABS (I): SIBAWAIHI

'Whoever wants to write about grammar after Sibawaihi let him feel humble!' [Mazini]

'About 50 years ago, I studied Sibawaihi's grammar in an advanced Arabic course and was much intrigued' [Chomsky]

INTRODUCTION

Sibawaihi's *al-Kitab* is the first grammar of Arabic. It is religiously motivated as far as content is concerned. It was devised to describe the language of the Holy Qur'an. Its form is most poetic trying to 'marry the beautiful to the useful.' This is seen in the use of terms such as *bab* 'Gate [of the Castle of Grammar]' rather than chapter, *shams* 'sun' feature rather than coronal, *cilah* letters for glides (semi vowels), etc.

Al-Kitab has earned much applause world-wide to the extent that French André Roman [University de Lyon II] used to say: 'We must stand up by respect when recalling what Sibawaihi and (his teacher) Khalil have left us in phonetics alone!' Sibawaihi's name itself is poetic viz. 'apple-smell'. His book is known as al-Kitab i.e. 'The Book!'

In the preliminaries of his book, Sibawaihi determines the categories of Arabic as a trilogy: N, V and P only. He defines what is *Hasan* good [acceptable] and what is *qabih* 'bad' such as 'I drank the sea, I carried the mountain, I came tomorrow and will come yesterday'. He tackles to the essential keys of Arabic grammar [and would influence all Arabic grammar after him viz. **transformation** and **government**. There is a gate of the V that transits to zero, one, two, etc. objects.

Other gates concern the transitivity of verbs and transformation viz. the gate of essence and accident e.g. *Yaa Allah!* 'O! God!'

1. SOUND SYSTEM

1.1. SOUND OUTLETS

Sibawaihi divides the speech tract into four sections which are pharynx, tongue, lips and nasal cavity. Each of which is then divided into far, middle and front. The pharynx produces 6 sounds /alif, ʔ, c, H, h, c, R/. The tongue [active articulator] produces various sounds. The lips produce /b, m, w/ the nasal cavity [light] n. the vowels seem to be absent [?]. Then he moves to the distinctive features.

1.2. DISTINCTIVE FEATURES

Sibawaihi defines <u>a set of [binary] distinctive features</u> such as voice, stop, lateral, nasal, roll, vowel, velarized, etc. voiceless sounds are gathered in fa Hatthahu shaXSun sakat 'someone urged him so he kept silent'. Coronal is called shams 'sun letters' by opposition to moon [-coronal].

1.3. PHONOLOGICAL PROCESSES

Sibawaihi deals with phonetic transformations such as assimilation as for the article ʔal- with its neighboring sound, whether it is +coronal or −

coronal. He deals with the behavior of feminine /t/ and /k/ sounds in end-boundary as in *qa:lat* Fatimah 'Fatima said' *shbish?* 'whassup?' It can be deleted in the noun [turned into /h/] but is kept in verb. [clitic][feminine]

Assimilation of labio-nasal nb into mb in *camber* 'amber' [regressive assimilation]. Most assimilations are regressive *ash-shams* 'the sun'. Progressive assimilation is found in examples such as *ʔimdaHHilalan* 'praise crescent'. Loan words such as *pirind* [sword][Farsi] are spirantized [Chomsky and Crystal] since Arabic lacks p/v it becomes *firind*.

The canonical syllable structure in Arabic is CV. Some instances that seem to disturb this are remedied by the insertion of a vowel as in *aHadun+ALLAH* 'one Allah' nl → nil. The reverse happens. Too many CV syllables in succession is not *Xiffa* 'light theory' [one of the theories of Arabic sound system] as in **yaDaraba* 'he is hitting' restructured into *yaDribu* CVCCVCV.

2. NON-CONCATENATIVE MORPHOLOGY

Nouns are considered as the origin 'asl' of lexical items ficl [verb]. Verbs are said to be derived from noun [as they are tense less, simple, kernel]. The noun can undergo morphological transformations i.e. deletion [final truncation], substitution, etc.

Both noun and verb in Arabic are based on a trilateral root C-C-C which [Robins 1967] denotes a general meaning, which is then converted into different words [] by the insertion of melodies and then transformations may operate such as imperfective, causative *nazzala* 'bring down', sick, etc. the most 'popular' transformation in textbooks of Arabic grammar is imperfective. It follows the lines of at least three analogies which can be found in examples such as *qatala* 'kill' *Daraba* 'hit' *Hasiba* 'think'. Their respective patterns are:

'he did'	'he will do':
facila	yafculu
facala	yafcilu
facial	yafcalu

The central vowel seems to play a crucial role in determining the pattern of the imperfective verb. These analogies are extremely productive.

Sick verb [including glides] are turned from one to the other [for lightness sake] *wacada* 'he promised'. Bare verb/basic can be 'clothed' as it were increased by the addition of one or more redundancy [Ibn Malik, cf. *Three Good Traditions*] letter found in sentence *saʔaltumu:ni:ha:* 'you asked me for her' e.g. *ʔadkhala* 'make enter' also realized [causative] by a doubling of central consonant *dakhkhala* 'ask enter.'

3. TRANSFORMATIONAL SYNTAX

Arabic is supposedly a V.S.O. language 'tested Abraham', 'who hit your father?' In fact its syntax is much more elaborate as it allows more than one word-order VSO, SVO, VOS, etc. It displays a double sentence structure [cop-drop] i.e. nominal and verbal sentences.

As far as nominal sentence structure is concerned, it starts by a subject directly followed by a predicate [cop-drop]. Carter (1968) believes that I.C.A. can apply to it. It's quite hazy *hatha ʔaXu:ka* 'this [is] your brother.'

Case plays a crucial role in determining word-order as well as thematic relations in a sentence as in *man Daraba ʔaXu:ka* 'who hit your brother?' Nominative is marked by u while accusative is marked by a [Triton 1977]. It turns from agent to patient with an inversion of theta roles with object.

Transformations are essentially used for semantic or pragmatic reasons/interpretation. Verbs such as *ʔisʔali Lqaryata* 'ask the village' can only be interpreted by postulating the existence of a deletion transformation such as 'ask the people of the village' so as to satisfy the requirements of selectional restrictions.

Sibawaihi first considers the canonical nominal sentence structure which consists of subject plus predicate []. In fact Arabic displays two major sentence [minor sentence] structures viz. nominal and verbal [with interchange].

The sentence can have two readings depending on the case of the object. It could either question *man Daraba ʔaXa:ka* 'who hit your brother' or *man Daraba ʔaXu:ka* 'whom did your brother hit?' with who agent . Case determines the whole LF of the sentence [cf. Chomsky 1997] With who agent by case ending of *ʔaXu:ka* 'your brother.' **u** nominative agent and **a** accusative patient.

Transformation [movement] are used for focus [as the major theme of the proposition] as in *ʔijja:ka nacbudu* 'Thee alone we worship' in which worship is excluded except for one viz. God.

Transformations are considered a necessary tool of interpretation of sentences. Since sentence *ʔisʔali Lqaryata* 'you ask the village' breaks selectional restrictions. You do not ask a village since village is [-human]. Sibawaihi postulates the existence of a deep structure of the form *ʔisʔali ʔahla lqaryati* 'ask the people of the village,' and then a deletion transformation which yields the above sentence. Likewise for the verse *makru llayli wa nnahar* 'the plotting of day and night.' In some sentences, Sibawaihi noted an alternation of case [passivization of intransitives]. Either the first NP is nominative and the last accusative or vice versa. Both are acceptable *si:ra* 'travelled' [cf. Chomsky 1981]

Besides transformation, Government is another key notion in Arabic grammar. Arabic grammarians have dealt with it extensively. They have established a government hierarchy, conflict and power. Government usually requires sisterhood plus adjacency?

It determines case and theta relations. Each category has its own government properties. As far as hierarchy is concerned the verb is considered as the top governor since it can govern a large number of arguments/NPs. It can assign [] two Cases [], it can allow movement of its own objects and even deletion without losing its governing power. This is illustrated respectively in in *ʔiyya:ka nacbudu* 'Thee alone we worship' and *kilayhima wa tamran* 'both plus dates.'

Conflict in government occurs when two governors dispute the same governee, one trying to assign nominative and one accusative to it. Ultimately the closest [adjacent] as *Darabtu wa Darabani Zaid* 'I hit and was hit by Zaid' *ʔinna Allah* 'lo! Allah...'

Inflection richness allows the shift SVO/VSO as in *qa:la qawmuka/qawmuka qa:lu*: 'your people said/said your people' as noted in Chomsky's Minimalist Program.

ARABS (II): IBN JINNI

ARABIC

Arabic is a **Semitic** language together with Hebrew and Aramaic. (Wright, 1979). At the present time, it is the Lingua Franca of the Arab World (Muslim World?). The word 'Arab' like the word 'Hebrew' were used originally to describe "passers-by" i.e. nomads traveling in search of better lands for their cattle in the desert. Now-a-days the Arab world stretches from Morocco in the west to Iraq in the east, where it is the state language. The Arabic language is a state of Diglossia, i.e. a high Arabic al-Fusha ('Clear Arabic') and a number of national dialects. Formal Literary Arabic, Classical Arabic, Modern Standard Arabic are all, referred to as al-Fusha.

ARABIC AND ISLAM

Classical Arabic (CA) is the language of ancient Arabic poetry (The 7 Poems). Starting from the 6th century, it has become primarily the language of the **Holy Koran** (see Muhammad Marmaduke Pickthall). It is the language of Islam *par excellence*. Most of the world's Muslims do not speak Arabic as their native language, but many can read the Koranic script and recite the Koran. Among non-Arab Muslims, translations of the Koran are usually accompanied by the original Arabic text.

THE STRUCTURE OF ARABIC

Arabic has a special verb morphology, as can be found, with more or less accuracy in the other Semitic languages (Hebrew and Aramaic). It consists of a set of **non-concatenative** techniques for the building of words from roots (Robins 1967). The root consists of discontinuous stretch of, usually three consonants to which a discontinuous set of (usually two) vowels is inserted to obtain words. For instance the root *k-t-b* which carries a general idea of writing. It needs the insertion of the discontinuous vowel pattern *a-a* to yield the words: *kataba* 'he wrote' *katabat* 'she wrote' *katabta* 'you wrote'. (Palmer 1985) (Ibn Malik '*bi faclala…*'). Many patterns are possible (see Ibn Jinni's Derivational transformations). Usually the addition of pronominal clitic pronouns at the end completes the 'Arabic one-word-sentence', as in: *ʔakal-tu* 'I ate'.

LIFE

Originally **Greco-Roman**, one-eyed Ibn Jinni (of his full name Uthman Ibn Jinni), was born in Mosul (Iraq). He started teaching Arabic morphology at a very early age, then was tutored by many scholars, the most notorious of which was Abu Ali Farisi, himself a student of renown Sibawaihi, the champion of Basra. The student followed his teacher to many parts of the Middle East, notably Iran, Iraq and Present-day Syria, for some 40 years. He was an eager student of Arabic grammar; recording his teacher's lessons besides listening and recording the speech of the Bedouins of Arabia. He was very proud of his new religion and language. After attaining fame, the teacher and the student were invited to several Emirs courts. At one occasion, Ibn Jinni met with famous poet **Mutanabi**. According to historian Yaqut, their friendship proved to be excellent and long-lasting. The poet gave free hand to the linguist to interpret his divans to the extent that he praised him for 'discovering meanings in his poems that he himself did not expect. The poet described Ibn Jinni as: "that's a man whose value is unknown to many." After the death of his teacher Ibn Jinni took over the Arabic chair at Mosul, until he himself passed away and was buried beside his teacher (1002).

BOOKS

Ibn Jinni's major works are *al-Khasais* and *sir sinacat al-irab*. He left some 50 books dedicated to the '**Arabic noble language**', as he called it. He mainly dealt with the phonetics, phonology and morphology of Arabic. In his book *sir sinaca* (the secret of parsing!!!), he describes the vowels and consonants of Arabic, their characteristics, classification, the nature of the segments (strong and weak), assimilation, metathesis, substitution and other phonetic transformations. His book *tafsir al-Muluk* (Kings' Morphological Transformations) is a treaties of detailed derivation processes in which he analyses the (simple and complex) morphological forms of Arabic verbs and nouns. In *al-Khasais*, he deals with the grammatical principles, based on his study of the language of the Bedouins of Mosul (Iraq). It is his biggest book, which consists of some 162 chapters that summarize his enormous Arabic linguistic knowledge. He is also the author of numerous commentaries on the works of Ali Al-Farisi, a commentary on Mazini's *tasrif* (Mazini's Morphology). He wrote commentaries on Mutabi's poetic divans. Besides being a master of Arabic phonetics, morphology, syntax and semantics, Ibn Jinni was also a literary man and a poet.

THEORIES

The most important theories of Ibn Jinni are **transformation**, derivation, analogy, argument, etc. As an example of syntactic transformation, he gives the example of the Koranic verse: "And ask the village", which has the input (and meaning): "ask (the people) of the village." A deletion transformation has taken place. Generally speaking, transformations can also apply by addition or compensation, etc. (cf. Sibawaihi). As far as *ishtiqaq* 'morphological derivation' is concerned, Ibn Jinni distinguishes two types: Minor and Major derivations. As an example of minor derivation, from the root s-l-m, you can derive *silm* 'peace', *salam* 'security', etc. (Robins 1967) Major derivation may start from a root such as k-l-m, to derive the words such as: *kallama* 'to hit', *malaka* 'to possess', etc.

As for the connection between **"expression and meaning"** Ibn Jinni believes in a strong almost natural relationship between the two sides of the "linguistic coin" To support his theory, he gives examples of verbs describing the sounds made by the wind, the birds, the ways of eating, etc., in which the sounds seem to mirror the actions.

Although Ibn Jinni's contribution in the field of Arabic philology is enormous, in fact he devoted himself mainly to the study of grammar, proving a major interest in lexicon and morphology without forgetting semantics and pragmatics.

Ibn Jinni is seen as the highest authority in the field of the linguistic discipline known as *tasrif* (morphological derivation). He is also considered as the founder of the science of *al-IShtiqaq al-akbar* (etymology). As a philologist, he has occupied a middle position between the two famous schools of Arabic linguistics of his time Kufa and Basra, based on *samac* 'attested data' and *qiyas* 'analogy', respectively. He eventually took the middle position of the **Baghdadi** School.

SEMANTICS

Ibn Jinni's work is usually associated with Arabic phonology and morphology. In fact, Ibn Jinni must also be associated with semantics, especially in his theory of *tasaqub* ('**onomatopoeia**'). The Arabic language is one of the many languages that have been the focus of extensive semantic studies. In fact, the study of Arabic has contributed much to semantics. It all stemmed from the huge work devoted to *tafsir* 'the interpretation the Holy Quran." Some also attribute much semantic work to Ibn Jinni's works as can be found in his books *al-muhtasab, al-khasais, al-munsif* in which he discusses certain social semantics problems i.e. 'pragmatics' to use the modern terminology as opposed to grammatical semantics.

Ibn Jinni was not just a philologist of Arabic, he was a philosopher of language.

10. HEBREWS

According to David Téné (1995), Biblical Hebrew (henceforth, BH) became an independent discipline relatively late, around the tenth century AD. Sad Fayumi's (882-942) work is considered the 1st grammar and dictionary of Hebrew. From the Christian side, the work on Hebrew started in the sixteenth century and was included in European curricula, thanks to scholars such as Johann Reuchlin (1506), among others.

In fact, the beginning of Jewish studies of Hebrew can be traced back to the **Golden Era** of Andalusia eighth to tenth century AD. The *Midrash* (literally 'examination') started rather late. The Jews did not write about BH due to religious, political or simply technical reasons.

Semitic languages have a peculiar morphology (Robins 1967) in which a single word combines a lexical root (consonants) and a grammatical pattern (vowels):

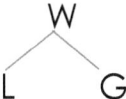

Ancient Hebrew texts, like Arabic, consisted of consonants only. No vowels were available and therefore no grammatical description was possible. Later *Masoretes* (Rabbinic literature) efforts were made in Palestine and Babylon, that started to provide the voweling for the HB. In the 9th century Ben Asher provided fully vocalized BH. "By 1050 it (Hebrew linguistics) reached its culmination in the words of Yehuda Hayyuj, Jonah Ben Janah and Samuel ha-Nagid. Once the BH text had been fully and finally vocalized, Hebrew linguistics did not embark on the painstaking route of inventing a descriptive method. Instead, they borrowed it wholesale from the Arab grammarians. As BH and classical Arabic are cognate languages, these early grammarians had only to adapt the Arabic descriptive method to the specific features of BH and to the linguistic situation of the Arabic-speaking Jews. The borrowing of the Arabic descriptive method is linked with the personality of Saadiya Gaon (882-942) born in Pithon, Egypt, he lived in Tiberias and became head of the rabbinical academy of Sura (near Baghdad). He was the greatest Jewish scholar in the tenth century."

Other top Jewish linguists and philosophers must be mentioned, such as Ibn Janah and Spinoza.

IBN JANAH (990-1050)

Rabbi Jonah, as he was known in Andalusia, is probably the most famous medieval Hebrew linguist (grammarian and lexicographer). He is considered as the father of Hebrew syntax. He is also accredited with establishing the rules for the intricate exegesis of the Old Testament, clarifying its most problematic passages.

First engaged in a career of medicine, he was soon moved by his strong Jewish convictions to the study of Biblical Hebrew. He devoted all his energy and time to the study of the sacred language of the Old Testament. In this sense, he can be considered as the first staunch 'scientific linguist' of Hebrew. His first book known as, *al-Mustalhaq* ("The Complement"), was written in Arabic like the rest of his works. It contained a critical review of the previous work done on verb morphology by Judah ben David Huyui, the founder of Hebrew grammar.

This critical work of Ibn Janah draw him the bitterness and animosity of the zealous and partisan students of Hayui. These disputes are to be found recoded in Ibn Janah's major work Kitab *at-tanqih* ("book of corrections"). This work of his consists of two parts. The first part is devoted to Hebrew lexicon, affixation and noun (case) inflections. It also contains an important and unsurpassed section on Hebrew syntax.

The second part of this book is devoted to Hebrew lexicon, in which he dealt with word morphology, explaining root patterns. Again much comparison is made with Arabic, helping him to show the meaning of words. This dual approach helped him in his exegesis, so as to clarify the obscure and difficult passages of the Old Testament.

BARUCH SPINOZA (1632-1677)

"Also known as Portuguese Bento De Espinosa is a Dutch-Jewish philosopher, the foremost exponent of 17th-century Rationalism."

"Spinoza's grandfather and father were Portuguese and had been crypto-Jews after the Spanish Inquisition had compelled them to embrace Christianity. Later, after Holland's successful revolt against Spain and the granting of religious freedom, they found refuge in Amsterdam."

"His studies so far had been mainly Jewish, but he was an independent thinker and had found more than enough in his Jewish studies to wean him from orthodox doctrines and interpretations of Scripture; moreover, the tendency to revolt against tradition and authority was much in the air in the 17th century. But the Jewish religious leaders in Amsterdam were fearful that heresies (which were no less anti-Christian than anti-Jewish) might give offence in a country that did not yet regard the Jews as citizens."

"The Jewish authorities, after trying vainly to silence Spinoza with bribes and threats, excommunicated him in July 1656, and he was banished from Amsterdam for a short period by the civil authorities."

"In May 1670 Spinoza moved to The Hague, where he remained until his death. He began to compose a Hebrew grammar, *Compendium Grammatices Linguae Hebraeae*, but did not finish it; instead, he returned to the *Ethica*, although the prospect of its publication became increasingly remote. There were many denunciations of his *Tractatus Theologico-Politicus* as an instrument "forged in hell by a renegade Jew and the devil." When the *Ethica* was completed in 1675, Spinoza had to abandon the idea of publishing it, though manuscript copies were circulated among his close friends."

11. HISTORICISM

Historical linguistics is a German affair.' It provided famous philologists such as Hermann Paul, Schleicher and the Grimms. The Grimm brothers were famous for their tales. Jacob Grimm became famous for his 'Great Vowel Shift' and 'Consonant Shifts.'

"German Grimm (1785-1863) described two important consonants shifts. They essentially concern nine consonants. One shift probably happened a few centuries before the Christian era. It affected the Indo-European consonants. This is evident in English, Dutch, Low German languages, and Old Norse. The other shift (about the 6th century AD) was less radical in scope and affected the Germanic consonants, resulting in the consonant system evident in Old High German and its descendants, Middle High German and modern High German (Standard German).

According to Grimm's law, the ancient unvoiced [p,t,k] became the English unvoiced [f,th,h]. The Old High German [f,d,h] led to correlations such as those found between the initial consonants of Greek [pod],

English [fod] and Old High German **spirant** stops [f,ts,kh]. Hence, the correlation between Latin [dou], English [two] and modern German [zwei](pronounced "tsvai"). Also, the originally voiced [bh,dh,gh] became the English voiced [b,d,g] and the Old High German [p,t,k]; compare with Sanskrit "bharati", English "bear" and upper German dialects of Old High German "ki-peran" (later standard German "ge-baren"). The Old High German examples show the second shift in addition to the first, which is seen in English." (...)

A REVIEW OF THE KING JAMES VERSION

The Bible consists of two sections, viz. The Old Testament (The Torah) and the New Testament (The Evangels). This is the oldest book in the world [1] and *the* best seller. Its original languages were Hebrew and Greek. It was translated into hundreds if not thousands of languages [...], including Latin (Jerome 4 AD), English (King James Version 1611) and Arabic. The Old Testament consists essentially of Moses' Pentateuch, while the New Testament consists essentially of the four canonical gospels plus the letters of St. Paul.

The usual attitude of the average Muslim towards this book is 'let me go and burn it!' and the same drastic attitude is found on the Christian side 'Muhammad? – the anti-Christ!' [sic.] In section, I feel somehow optimistic to try and bridge this gap – if not abyss.

This is a critical analysis of different aspects of the Bible as far as *contents* (...) and *language* are concerned (phonology, syntax, symbols, idioms, parables and stories). My major references will be the King James Version of the Bible (henceforth KJV) and the Contemporary English Version of the Bible (Henceforth CEV).

The English of the KJV is described in the back-cover as 'easy-to-read, self-pronouncing, favorite for almost four centuries (...) it brings the extraordinary power and poetry of Scripture into life.' As far as I am concerned, KJV is not easy-to-read as it shows of a few linguistic idiosyncrasies in terms of its phonetics, syntax, story-telling, etc.

Let us begin with a story, 'the Story of David' in 1 Kings 1:1: "Now King David was old and *stricken in years;* and they covered him with clothes, but he *gat* no heat. Wherefore his servants said unto him, *let there be sought for my lord* the king a young virgin: and let her stand before the king, and let her cherish him, and let her lie in thy bosom, that me lord king may get heat. So they sought for a fair *damsel* throughout all the coasts of Israel, and found Abishag a Shunammite, and brought her to the king. And the damsel was very fair, and *cherished* the king, and *ministered to* him: but the king knew her *not.*"

This story poses a few social and linguistic problems. The enormous difference in age between a 'very old man' and a 'very young damsel' may be considered as illegal in some secular countries. David was so old that he was cold all the time in spite of all the blankets they put on him, in the warm climate of the Middle East! He had reached senile age with all its effects of impotence, in some Bible versions (he could not have sex with her) and amnesia (he did not know her). He was so old that he could not even go to the coronation feat of his beloved son Solomon. From his bed, he ordered that his son should ride his mule for recognition.

As far as linguistic idiosyncrasies are concerned, you may have noticed that KJV language is rich and interesting. It was written in so-called Modern English, i.e. Shakespearean English. The difference between this language and Contemporary English poses a few problems to the linguist.

If language is the goal and focus of all linguists, the schools and approaches to this subject are many, viz. Structuralism, functionalism and philology (also known as diachronic linguistics). A German philologist of the 18th c. called Jacob Grimm has suggested a linguistic mechanism known after his name as Grimm's Law, to try and deal with the historical development of ancient languages.

To explain philological transformations such as those found in KJV, Grimm's Law which is concerned with consonants, side-by-side with the 'Great Vowel Shift' is suggested. To understand these two theories, one may humorously quote the Mad Tea Party in which each guest is asked to move one place to the right. In language, there are natural tendencies to search for the easiest pronunciation possible i.e., the 'theory of the least effort'. This search for 'least effort' will raise a few problems in language development. Grimm's Law and the Great Vowel Shift (GVS) will try to explain them.

Historically, English belongs to a small linguistic family, i.e. Germanic family (which includes German, Scandinavian and Dutch) and to a bigger and higher family, known as Indo-European which also includes Sankrit, Hindi, Gujrati. So, this has tempted many linguists and philologists to try the reconstruction of the phonetic system of the mother language.

The Germanic branch of Indo-European has undergone certain phonetic transformations and thus caused the split between European and Eastern languages. Original phonemes such as [bh] [dh] [gh] became [b] [d] [g], became [p] [t] [k] and then became [f] [θ] [h]. The illustrative examples are:

Indo-European   English
Bhero   bear

Ghans	goose
Dekm	ten
Genos	kin
Pater	father
Treyes	three
Kornu	horn

The other set of phonetic transformations concerns the vowel system viz. 'GVS'. In this process, all long vowels lose two degrees in their tongue-height and are transformed in open mid-high diphthongs e.g. [i:] into [ay]:

Illustrative examples are:

Middle English	Modern English
na:m	neim 'name'
me:t	mi:t 'meat'
ri:d	raid 'ride'
bo:t	boat

In this story of 'push and drag!' front vowels such as [a] will be substituted for back vowels such as [o]. This is clearly noticeable in verse 'David gat no heat' (spelt with an [a]) and is found in American dollars motto 'In God we trust' (cf. Tyneside in England).

[see Ben Rochd, *Words* 2020 b]

Originally, English was a nebula of different languages, viz. Latin, Norse, German, French, etc. besides being divided into OLD, MIDDLE and

MODERN ENGLISH.

Latin left words such as 'Bible', 'Pope', 'London', German left 'men and women' (plurals in –*en*) by opposition to French plural-endings in –*s* e.g. 'table/table-s'. French also left 'cuisine terms' including 'mutton, beef, poultry'. In David's story we notice words such as 'damsel', 'cherished', 'minister' (someone to serve you!)

Among the syntactic features of KJV, the use of archaic pronouns such as 'thou', 'ye', etc. The use of obsolete linking words such as 'the, and, but', polysyllabic words such as 'stricken' (struck), 'unto' (to), auxiliary-subject inversion, e.g. 'Then shall the Kingdom of Heaven belikened unto ten virgins' for 'the kingdom of heaven shall be..' (Matthew 25). The use of passive as in 'let there be sought for my lord'. The use of relative clause such as *they that were foolish* for *the foolish ones.*' The use of **_italics_** for emphasis and capitalization inside the sentence after a comma or semi-colon. The use of end-negation 'he knew her not', instead of he did not know her'.

Among the stylistic features of KJV, we find the use of parables such as the Story of the Ten virgins (for modern 'girls') (see below). We find also the use of symbols such as 'camel', 'patching', 'fruit', 'song', etc. The 'camel entering the eye of the needle' illustrating the impossibility for a rich man to enter Heaven (Matthew 19:24). The ugliness of 'patching an old material with a new one', i.e. defending truth with falsehood: "No man putteth a piece of new cloth unto an old garment, for that which is put in to fill it up taketh from the garment, and the rent is made worse." (Matthew 9:16). In Matthew 21:43 we read: "Therefore say I unto you, The kingdom of God shall be taken from you, and given to a nation bringing forth the fruits thereof. In Isaiah 42:10 we read: "Sing unto the LORD a new song, and his praise from the end of the earth, ye that go down to the sea, and all that is therein; the isles, and the inhabitants thereof."

Idioms are also used for illustration. For example, when the Roman governor uttered: 'I wash my hands off it', he was expressing the end of his responsibility concerning the execution of Jesus, which was much wanted by the Jews. (Matthew 27:24).

AUGUST SCHLEICHER (1821-1968)

August Schleicher is a German linguist, who is largely considered as the culmination of historical (comparative) linguistics of the 19th century, which he directed and pioneered. As a student at the University of Tübingen, He adopted Hegel's philosophy, then later Darwinian evolution theory. His ultimate goal was to develop a logical theory of language based on Hegel's logic and Darwinian natural selection. From 1850 to 1857 he was a lecturer at the University of Prague, where he taught philology and comparative linguistics applied to the Greek and Latin. Then he turned to the study of Slavic languages. In 1852 he studied Lithuanian while living in Lithuania. This was a move from recorded texts to the study of live speech of speakers of an Indo-European language. The results of his research were published in his excellent book *Handbuch der litauischen Sprache* (1856). It was the first scientific and complete study of the Lithuanian language. Then moving to the University of Jena in 1857, he published his most famous book, *Der Vergleichenden Grammatik Der Indogermanischen Sprachen* (1962). This was the result of a study of Sanskrit, Greek and Latin, in an attempt to reconstruct the ancestral proto-Indo-European 'mother' of these languages.

Schleicher believed firmly in Darwinian natural selection. So, according to him, language could be equated with a biological species, the life of which was determined by the natural laws: birth, development and decline. His method was to group languages, as botanists do, into families and genealogical trees known as *Stammbaumtheorie* (a family tree theory). It was the key to the 'historical linguistics' approach.

12. SAUSSURE (1857-1913)

In the 19th c. Charles Darwin's ideas appeared, and were largely predominant in every field including language studies (cf. Historicism). Darwin had first tried to become a priest, then a doctor, then took a long trip to South America and Australia, where he studied many biological artefacts. He tried to establish a link between a chain of humans and that of animals, but was faced by a 'missing link.'

The man who broke with the Darwinian paradigm in language studies was Ferdinand de Saussure. For him language is a "social fact" rather than a biological tangible thing. Saussure was influenced by French Emil Durkheim's notion of the "collective mind" or German *Volkgeist*. Language stands in contrast with biological, physical, or even psychological facts (vs. Chomsky). It is an abstract but socially effective fact like "stones." ("**Hit me with your dagger and your sword, but not with your tongue and your word!**")

His full name Mongin Ferdinand de Saussure. He was born in Geneva (Switzerland) in 1857, from a

Huguenot family that had to flee the civil wars of sixteenth century France. His posthumous book *Cours de Linguistique Générale* (1916) is considered as the starting point of modern linguistics and himself as the father of synchronic linguistics. (He wrote a book *posthumous*; a genius (!)

He had successfully broken with 'Darwinian historicism', and laid the foundations for many developments of 20th century linguistics. He perceived linguistics as a branch of a general science of signs, he proposed to call semiology (vs. biology). (see Sampson 1980) His systematic re-examination of language is based on five assumptions:

A) The scientific study of language needs to develop and study the system rather than the history of linguistic phenomena.

B) The basic elements of language can only be studied in relation to their functions rather than in relation to their causes.

C) The relationship between the signifier and the signified is arbitrary.

D) Language is primarily a "social activity" (in some ways this is the most radical and yet least developed element of his system).

E) Language is socialized at every level, from the production of phonemes to the interpretation of complex meaning.

While still a student, Saussure established his reputation with a brilliant contribution to comparative linguistics, which he presented in his "Mémoire sur le système primitive des voyelles dans les langues indo-européennes" (1879). His name is affixed, however, to his book *Cours de linguistique générale* (1916), a reconstruction achieved posthumous by two of his students, Charles Bally and Albert Sechehaye. The publication of this work is frequently considered to be the starting point of 20th century modern linguistics.

Saussure defended that language must be considered as a social phenomenon. It is a structured system that can be viewed synchronically (as it exists at any particular point in time) v. diachronically (as it changes in the course of time). He also introduced two terms that have become common currency in linguistics *"parole"*, i.e. the speech of the individual person, and *"langue,"* i.e. a systematic, structured language, such as English, or French. His distinction proved to be the starting avenue of modern linguistic, or philosophical fashion known as STRUCTURALISM.

WHAT IS LANGUAGE?

To answer this anthological question, the answers were many. In the 19th c. the fashion was to try and equate "language" studies with biology; being influenced by Darwinian ideology. It was the case of German philologists such as Hermann Paul and Schleicher. It was given the biological analogy of species such as "carrots" or "cats".

For Saussure, the proper study of language should see "language" as a semiotic system at one given point in time, disregarding any historical dimension. It is similar to the game of chess. No history is relevant, in that game.

Although Saussure himself worked as a student in the historical field for the reconstruction of Indo-European languages, and even taught in the same frame in Geneva and Paris, he managed to see the relevance of the other approach. For the language user it is irrelevant to know about the evolution of, say, the English language from the time of Shakespeare, let alone Chaucer (that was closer to German than to modern English!) Today, all the speaker of English needs to know is how to use it properly. He can ignore its past (or even its structure). All he has to do is to be able to use it in accordance with what is intelligible to the people in Oxford Street (London), or any other speech community, for that matter!

Saussure is famous for his dichotomies: synchronic vs. diachronic, langue vs. parole, signifié vs. significant, paradigmatic vs. syntagmatic. Language is form (-imec) non-substance (-itic). That is a meaningful sign rather than a sound or a piece of ink on a piece of paper or chalk on the blackboard!

In STRUCTURALISM, each item (word or morpheme) of the system has no intrinsic value, but rather derives all its sense from its relations with the other items. It is its contrasts and dependencies with the other items, which is crucial. It is like a brick in the wall! No absolute value: 'you are not a 'good v. bad' person; it's your social relations that matter!'

The social fact can be exemplified by English Mister Maddox coming to the Moroccan university to teach wearing a skirt. No way (!) Although his neighbouring Scotsmen Mac. would put on the kilt without any fear or shame in his country. (!)

Saussure explains his **principles** as follows:

A) "Nous appelons **signe** la combinaison du concept et de l'image acoustiques" (p. 99)

B) « le signe linguistique est **arbitraire.** Ainsi l'idée de « Sœur » n'est liée par aucun rapport intérieur avec la suite de sons s-o-r qui lui sert de signifiant » (p. 100)

C) « **Etat de langue** ne peut être qu'approximative » (p. 143)

D) «Un groupement, les **paradigmes** de flexion : Enseignement- enseigner enseignons etc. clément justement changement etc. (p. 174)

E) "la langue existe dans la **collectivité** sous la forme d'une somme d'empreintes déposées dans chaque cerveau" (p. 38)

F) "le signe linguistique unit non une chose et un nom, mais un **concept** et une image **acoustique**" (p. 98)

G) "le **syntagme** se compose de deux ou plusieurs unités consécutives (par exemple : re-lire ; contre nous ; la vie humaine, Dieu est bon." (p.170)

H) "la linguistique **diachronique** « étudie, non plus les rapports entre termes coexistants d'un état de langue, mais entre termes successifs qui se substituent les uns aux autres dans le temps" (p. 193)

I) "l'objet de la linguistique **synchronique** générale est d'établir les principes fondamentaux de tout système idiosychronique, les facteurs consécutifs de tout état de langue. » (p. 141)

J) « Etat de langue ne peut être qu'**approximatif.** » (p. 143)

(de Saussure 1985 *Cours de linguistique générale*)

13. COPENHAGEN

'The simplicity we look for in a scientific theory is something like fewness of elementary concepts employed; and in this respect Lamb beats Chomsky hands down' (Sampson 1980)

Language X stays language X whether it is spoken, written or transmitted by Morse. According to Saussure, language is 'structure non substance'. The sounds belong to the physical world (acoustic) and the concepts belong either to the physical world or to the logical world. The sound repertoire and the concepts repertoire are unstructured. Each language imposes its proper structure on them. Arabic for instance lacks the /v/ sound, /s/ and / s/ are contrastive, whereas /b/ and /p/ are not. In English *cousin* expresses the relations of 'son of uncle', 'daughter of uncle', 'son of aunt', and 'daughter of aunt'. No contrast!

GLOSSEMATICS is a theory and system of linguistic analysis proposed by the Danish scholar Louis Hjelmslev (1899-1965) and his collaborators, who were strongly influenced by the work of Swiss linguist Ferdinand de Saussure who claims that 'language is form non-substance'. Hjelmslev in his turn distinguished the form and the substance of language in expression/form-expression/content.

According to Hjelmslev, language branches into form and substance on the one hand, and content and expression on the other. These levels combine to yield four 'strata' (layers): substance-content, substance-form, expression-form and expression-content. The extremes do not belong to language.

[see Ben Rochd *Words* 2020 b]

This is a pure theory. American Sidney Lamb (1929-) had tried to make it more concrete by applying it to English. The word LOCOMOTE for instance can be realized as *go or move*, which make up a 'sememe'. Likewise *under and beneath* (lower position) are alternative realizations of the same semantic element 'lower than'. We can use either one. This is what Lamb calls 'or-relation'. 'Or-relation' is opposed to 'and-relation.' 'Undergo' (submit) for instance consists of 'under' (lower position) and 'go' (move). It is what he calls 'and-relation.'

The 'relation portmanteau' is realized when verb 'go' for instance is combined to 'the first person singular present' to yield 'I go.' It is 'and-relation' and is represented by a triangle, whereas the 'or-relation' is represented by an upside down parenthesis.

[ibid]

Or again:

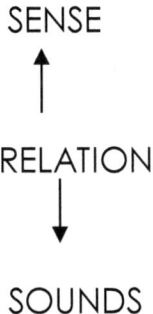

SENSE

RELATION

SOUNDS

A lexeme like garçon is a portmanteau for the sense units MALE, YOUNG and HUMAN on the one hand, and the units of sound /g/ /a//r//s//ɔ□/ on the other.

Sidney Lamb's theory can find support from new discoveries in computing and aphasia (see glossary). It is based on the 'item and arrangement' approach. Still, In spite of all his efforts to make Hjelmslev's glossematic theory more concrete, American Lamb could not keep up with the Chomskyian school as he based his approach on 'item and arrangement', whereas Chomsky based his on 'item and process.'

Although, Sampson's verdict is that Hjelmslev's idea is a good one, it is unpractical.

Hjelmslev's Glossematics may be regarded as the Saussurean emphasis on **form** vs. **substance** in the 'content plane' (semantics and grammar) and in the 'expression plane' (phonology), and on the definition of form as the interpretations of elements, both carried to their logical extremes; that is to say, content analysis must be independent of extra-linguistic existential criteria, and expression analysis (phonology) must be independent of (assumed extra-linguistic) phonetic criteria. Relations between elements, not the elements themselves, are the object of a science, and only by keeping this strictly to the fore can the Saussurean ideal of an autonomous linguistics, not dependent on any other discipline, be realized. The two planes are each regarded as analyzable into ultimate constituents (e.g. *mare* into m, e, ə or m, a, r, e, on the plane of expression, and into 'horse', 'female', 'singular', on the plane of content). They are not isomorphous, as no connection can be drawn between the individual phonemes or letters and the minimal elements of content; but both planes are to be analyzed in an analogous way, and each is co-ordinate and equivalent in a language system. It is precisely this claim to equivalence between the two planes that others have found difficult to accept, since differences in expression are independently observable in a language and belong to a strictly circumscribed field, whereas differences in semantic content (which is limitless) are only revealed through differences in expression in a language.

Glossematics is a system of linguistic analysis based on the distribution and interrelationship of glossemes, the smallest meaningful units of a language –e.g., a word, a stem, a grammatical element, word order, or intonation.

According to Lamb, each word is a symbol and is a PORTMANTEAU for sound and meaning, e.g. *boy* is /b+o+i/ and [+human+male+adult].

Generally speaking, language connects the messages (semantics) to pronunciation (phonetics). Language offers alternates (or-relation) but the speaker has to choose those which are compatible with the successively larger units. For instance /l/ in Arabic can be either clear or dark depending on the preceding vowel, respectively by /i/ or /a/ and /u/ as in *billahi* v. *wallahi*!

When comparing this theory with Chomsky's enterprise, he seems to side with Lamb. He states 'Lamb's treatment of meaning is no worse, though it is no better, than Chomsky's.' (Sampson, 1980) 'Chomskyan linguists have been forced to recognize the existence of what have been 'conspiracies', in the sense that the outputs of a given bloc of rules manifest patterning which is present neither in the inputs to that bloc of rules nor in the rules themselves (Soams and Perlmutter 1970). 'Lamb and Chomsky agree in seeing a language as linking 'semantic representations' –messages- with 'phonetic representations' –pronunciation.

14. PRAGUE

"The Prague linguistic circle" founded as "Cèrcle Linguistique de Prague," became known around the world as the Prague School. It included Russian émigrés such as Roman Jakobson, Nikolay Trubetzkoy, and Sergei Karecevskiy, as well as the famous Czech literary scholars Rene Wellek and Jan Mukarovsky. Among its founders was the eminent Czech linguist Vilem Mathesius (president of PLC until his death in 1945)."

"Its proponents developed methods of structural literary analysis during the years 1928-39. It has had significant continuing influence on linguistics and semiotics. After World War II, the circle was disbanded but the Prague School continued as a major force in linguistic functionalism (distinct from the Copenhagen school or English Firthian – later Hallidean linguistics)."

1. PRAGUE

Some people consider the Prague school as more interesting than even Chomsky himself! The word "Prague", pronounced differently /prag/ and /preig/, is the name of a city, that was the capital of Czechoslovakia. It was behind the **Iron Curtain**. If you say "Prague" many minds automatically go to what is known as the (bloody) 'Prague Spring' or '**le Printemps de Prague**': that is the time when the Russian army invaded Prague in the sixties to crash its democratic attempts.

As far as linguistics is concerned, Prague stands for a special philosophy of language. It is sometimes more philosophical than linguistic. Take for instance STRUCTURALISM; it's not just a linguistic approach. It's also a philosophy, not to say an ideology. For some people it's the answer to life. Structuralism is a conception of life, and likewise FUNCTIONALISM.

Unlike Saussure who stood alone as the initiator of structuralism, the Prague school consisted of many imminent linguists who came to make the Prague school of linguistics. One should mention the founder of that school the Czech MATHESIUS, the major figure of that school who is the Russian prince Nicolai

TRUBETZKOY, another Russian, who has turned American Roman JAKOBSON (pronounced /yakobson/), the French linguist André MARTINET and finally the native American William LABOV (/shwa, back stressed vowel/). As far as linguistic conception and philosophy are concerned, Prague does not stand for anything local. Different people from different nationalities have cooperated to make this school. Or to put it differently all those scholars who shared the same view and the same method came into being a school called Prague even when they were originally thousands of miles apart.

Once more one has to refer to Saussure as he is considered 'the father of modern linguistics', since he has influenced all those who came after him. Saussure considers language to be a social fact. Language is the fruit of society; but Saussure is solely interested in language; the way language is made. Society is, to take another metaphor, "the mother of language" but Saussure's interest is in the "baby" only. For the people of Prague, all students of Saussure, the interest is in both. They consider language as the fruit of society but are also interested in knowing the role played by language in society. [LANGUAGE and PEOPLE].

Prague people looked at the function, the 'use' of language in addition to its 'shape' and 'structure'. While Saussure looked at language as a system, Prague added two other dimensions. They took into consideration people and literature, i.e. the social, and the poetic functions with Roman Jakobson.

Let's consider now the Prague people and see their respective contributions.

This school was founded by Mathesius who was Czech. The main thing attributed to him is the consideration of the 'use' beside and in addition to the 'structure'. So, a sentence is not simply a syntactic structure; it is used to inform people or to mislead them as it were. Mathesius' famous concept was known as FUNCTIONAL SENTENCE PERSPECTIVE (F.S.P. for short). What does that mean? Take, for instance, a sentence like *Bush has come back*. This sentence brings some (piece of) information. But not all of it is new to you. Half of it is already known to you and hence the laughter. *Bush* is known but what is new is the second half of the sentence *has come back*.

So, for a structuralist, it is simply the structure of a sentence; for Mathesius it is divided into two halves the old knowledge and the new one. The thing known already is called THEME whereas the new piece of information is called RHEME ('Topic' and 'comment'; 'Makhbaru bihi' and 'Mukhbaru ᶜanhu'). Of course you need the theme before you can benefit of the information of the rheme. The theme and rheme are like the table and the cup of coffee: you can't put your cup, unless you have a table. So in the case of *Bush*, suppose I took another name, a name you did not know you would not benefit of the information *has come back*. Again now that you know that *Bush* has come back, I could add something else and *departed as soon as he had landed*. So in this case the whole first sentence would be the 'theme' and the second sentence *departed as soon as he had landed* would be the 'rheme'.

Now the PASSIVE construction is seen neutrally by a structuralist, but is it so really? Usually, when the government of some country wants to raise the price of some products much needed by the people they do not say: the minister of economy has decided to raise the prices. They put it in the passive: the prices of sugar, bread, milk, etc... will be raised by 10% starting from next January. So the passive is not just a structure. It plays a role; namely it saves the minister's life.

The second figure major linguist of Prague was Prince Nicolai Trubetzkoy. His father was the dean of a Russian University. He fled from Russia after Lenin took the power. He joined Mathesius in Prague and besides doing linguistics he was doing militancy. At that time Hitler and the Nazis were persecuting the Jews. So Trubetzkoy who was an outspoken adversary of Nazism, was tortured to death by the Gestapo. He managed to finish his most important book a short time before dying. This important book is known as the Trubetzkoy's *Principles of Phonology*. Trubetzkoy draws a distinction between 3 types of functions in phonology: DEMARCATIVE FUNCTION, DISTINCTIVE FUNCTION and EXPRESSIVE FUNCTION.

First, the distinctive function: some items play a distinctive function. Take for example, the three vowels /i e o/; they would play a distinctive function once inserted in the syntagm [p—t]. They would distinguish for us between three words. They are *pit, pet, pot* . Remember signifié is a 'concept' not a 'concrete thing': and the PHONEME, as an abstract concept, belongs to LANGUE; whereas the SPEECH SOUND, which is concrete belongs to PAROLE. We can see that this function namely -- the DISTINCTIVE one -- is carried further by Roman Jakobson's 'DISTINCTIVE FEATURES'.

To explain the DEMARCATIVE FUNCTION, usually, to drink must be done properly. You drink slowly, bit by bit. You don't just pour a jug into your stomach. You empty the glass little by little. As the glass is being emptied your stomach is being filled, little by little. In speech, the same thing happens between the speaker and the hearer. If you are speaking you should respect certain pauses, certain stress patterns, certain sentence rhythm otherwise you would say things like *dothiko.* I remember a girl who spoke like that. What she wanted to say is *I don't think so!* You can't understand her, because there isn't enough demarcation in her speech. The opposite could also happen. You may have noticed that some people speak like this: *hhm let see, I mean.* This self-demarcation gives the speaker time to prepare his utterance.

Finally, the EXPRESSIVE FUNCTION of language, or what Le Page calls Acts of Identity. It means that you have a correlation between different linguistic items and different social considerations. There are relationships between certain linguistic paradigms and certain social facts. Take for instance, the paradigm /au eu iu/ and take the word *house*. We know, that in RP it is pronounced with [au]. But once you go to England, you find that every social group speaks a 'different' language. Some would pronounce it with /au/, some with /eu/, and finally some with /iu/. The lower your pronunciation in the paradigm (scale for London) the lower your social status. This fact reminds us of Bernard Shaw's Pygmalion. Another expressive function of language was noticed by Trubetzkoy in the Mongolian language (Mongolia been a country squeezed between Russia and China). In the Mongolian language, there is a difference between the speech of the two sexes. Back vowels in male speech correspond to front vowels in female speech. As I know no Mongolian, I will use an example from English. Take for instance, the sentence *I was by the door*. It contains the vowels /a/, / o/, /a/ again, and finally /o/. In the female speech they would be replaced by their front counterparts /a/ → /i/ and /e/ respectively.

So we can see that different linguistic items express different social facts.

Roman Jakobson, is a very important figure in functional linguistics. His impact is found on both sides of the Atlantic Ocean. He started in Russia, then he went to work with Mathesius and Trubetzkoy in Prague and finished in America as a lecturer at l'Ecole Libre des Hautes Etudes in New York City, then at Harvard (the equivalent of Oxford in England).

Jakobson's fame is due to two major contributions: POETICS and UNIVERSAL GRAMMAR. Thanks to these two hypotheses, Jakobson had an immense impact on American scholarship. He first noticed the pragmatic mentality of Americans who look for material, concrete benefits so they have come to idealize science at the expense of arts. Some will tell you that in America, if you are in science and technology you can become rich; whereas if you are a painter, a writer, or a poet, you are doomed to starve. So you better be a physicist, a chemist or better a linguist (!)

To bring a remedy to this regrettable state of affairs, Jakobson proposed Poetics (which is different from stylistics as the latter deals with the different styles of the same language; whereas poetics deals with the aesthetic aspects of language) as a kind of marriage between science and arts, more precisely between linguistics and literature. Those working in poetics try to apply linguistic theories to the analysis of literary texts (see Haj. John Ross dealt with a poem about 'Jerusalem' and the advertisement of Coca Cola).

a coke and smile makes you feel nice makes me feel good ah; that's the way it should be o see the whole world smiling with me coca Cola adds life have a coke and smile

We suggest that this sequence should be divided and made into a poem:

Have coke and smile
Makes you feel nice
Makes me feel good

Ah; that's the way it should be

And I'd like to see

The whole world

Smiling with me

Coca cola adds life

Have a coke and smile

Notice the parallelisms in SOUND and WORD, e.g. ai which is found in smile, smiling and also the transformation (Nominalization): *smile* → *smiling*. The first one denoting life while the second is frozen and makes the action of smiling become a product of the capitalist system just like a coke. Have a coke and smile, i. e. the smile is parallel to the coke. Now if you join the parallelisms you obtain the visual image of the smile and that of the coke tin.

UNIVERSAL GRAMMAR on the other hand is a theory that suggests that all languages are cut to the same pattern. Jakobson applied it to phonology and Chomsky would apply it later to syntax. The latter benefited from him in phonology as well by using his theory of DINSTINCTIVE FEATURES. This was an important step in re-orienting linguistics in the USA. American descriptivists, before the advent of Jakobson, thought in terms of RELATIVISM and PHONEME. They thought that the phoneme was the smallest unit of language and that languages can vary endlessly.

For Jakobson, languages can vary indeed but within limits which he calls Universal Grammar. We may speak different languages. We may even use different sounds like Arabic /X/ or other sounds, which exist in certain languages but not in others; but still, we all have the same sound features like VELAR, FRICATIVE, STOP, etc. Languages may differ but they are like the fingers of the same hand, and hence the hypothesis of UNIVERSAL GRAMMAR. (UG)

Another argument in favour of UG is that unlike the American structuralists before him, who linked each language to its particular culture (Sapir-Whorf) and a social dimension, for Jakobson, LANGUAGE has to do with the psychology of the individual. Not only do we all share those features like labial, velar, etc.. which show the similarity of our vocal tract, but in fact what Jakobson wanted to demonstrate is much more sophisticated than that. He wanted to show the insight that goes beyond the vocal tract to the human mind. His twelve distinctive features have a psychological reality and are the same in all human beings. The human mind is the same for all human beings and this has consequences for the field of CHILD LANGUAGE, too.

A Moroccan child taken to China would come to acquire Chinese perfectly after a few years, the same for a Chinese child taken to England would acquire English as his mother-tongue, rapidly and uniformly.

As an example of 'distinctive features' approach, suppose I wanted to talk about somebody, you cannot tell 'who this person is?' since there are billions of people. Suppose now I made it more precise an 'English person'. Still not clear, there are some 70 million of them, an 'English teacher?' 'No!' 'an old English teacher?' There are thousands of them. An 'old English Teacher in our department

(O.University)?' Now, you know him... viz. 'Mister Maddox.'

In phonology (after the social example) one could take, say, six phonemes $X_1, X_2, X_3, X_4, X_5, X_6$: b m t d n l. What do we notice then? We notice that b is LABIAL, the difference between t and d is VOICE; so let's see whether these two properties are sufficient to distinguish our set of speech sounds.

	B	M	t	d	N	L
LABIAL	+	+	−	−	−	−
VOICE	+	+	−	+	+	+

These two features do not seem to help much. Of course, they have set the /t/ **sound** apart. But the others are not: the b and m are not distinguished yet and likewise for: d, n and l. Let's move to another trial by adding the features NASAL and continue until each item is different from all the others. Obviously you need more features.

	B	m	t	d	n	L
LABIAL	+	+	-	-	-	-
VOICE	+	+	-	+	+	+
NASAL	-	+	-	-	+	-

2. LONDON

England had some spelling reforms in the 16th century as the English were trying to make their National Language out of the multitude of unintelligible dialects they had at that time (cf. *eyren*). And this task required a very serious work in PHONETICS. One should also take into consideration, what was known in the nineteenth and beginning of the twentieth century as the BRITISH EMPIRE (up to the 1950s when the subjugated countries started becoming independent and made what is known as the COMMONWEALTH in association with Britain). The colonies of the British Empire consisted of countries like EGYPT, NIGERIA, SOUTH AFRICA, etc., in our continent. It also consisted of (parts of) CHINA, INDIA, IRAQ in Asia. Actually, it consisted of many countries and it stretched from MALAYSIA in the far-east to the

WEST INDIES in Central America Jamaica, Barbados, Trinidad, etc., (the place of Bob Marley).

One can easily imagine the number of languages available to the English linguists working at a school called S.O.A.S (School of Oriental and African Studies) which is a department in London College University; and hence the title 'LONDON SCHOOL'.

The people who made London School are Henry Sweet, Daniel Jones, J.R. Firth, Malinowski and Micheal Halliday. Henry Sweet and Daniel Jones were phoneticians, J.R. Firth dealt with phonology and semantics, Malinowski dealt with semantics and Halliday with syntax.

Henry Sweet was responsible for the PHONEME. He is the original of Professor Higgins in Bernard Shaw's *Pygmalion*. For some personal animosity, he never succeeded in having a job at S.O.A.S. as a lecturer in spite of his work and publications. His merits were recognized posthumous (after his death). Daniel Jones was responsible for the CARDINAL VOWEL SYSTEM, (i e a/u o ʌ) and the author of a very nice book called *Everyman's English Pronouncing Dictionary*. Both Sweet and Jones worked hard on the ENGLISH SPELLING REFORM, on SHORT HAND and I.P.A. (i.e. International Phonetic Alphabet).

J. R. FIRTH is the major figure of London School. He had a special approach to phonology; called PROSODIC. Prosodic phonology draws our attention to the fact that the approach based on the phoneme is misleading in phonetics (let alone normal spelling). The approach based on the phoneme is segmental, i.e. it divides speech into segments VCCV. But with some languages like Chinese (remember China was partly a British colony); this approach did not work satisfactorily (e.g. *nan*). As I do not know any Chinese, let us take the preposition, *on* in English. Obviously, it consists of two segments (alias two phonemes). What about the French impersonal pronoun *on*? Does it also consist of two phonemes? The segmental approach is misleading. In fact, it consists of only one vowel with a prosody (ɔ̃). We do not produce the /o/ vowel then the /n/ consonant, separately. In reality, we produce them together and the prosody is a 'help' of the vowel o. The nasal feature (represented by a diacritic) just 'colours' the vowel.

As a matter of fact, this is one of the idiosyncrasies of the French language.

In semantics, J.R. FIRTH questions -as far as the relationship between FORM and MEANING is concerned- the Saussurian notion of 'Arbitrariness'. For him, this relationship is not totally arbitrary. One could try and find the connection between form and meaning. Take, for instance, the words starting with the consonant cluster /sl/ in English. The words like *slave, slam, slain*. etc., all seem to share some kind of negative connotation (feature); namely 'violence'. The *slaves* were taken violently from their home-land. (Remember 'Roots'). To *slam* the door means to shut it violently and *slain;* to slay (/slei/) means to kill violently.

To take another example, this time from Arabic, consider the verb paradigm:

      sa:la   'drip'

      ma :la   'lean'

      ta :la   'be lasting'

They all seem to connote some kind of continuation of some sort. So it is not just the case of onomatopoeia, that justifies the strong link between form and meaning (see Ibn Jinni).

Malinowski, on his part, has mainly dealt with semantics. From Polish aristocratic descent, and one of those who escaped the Iron Curtain and came to live in the eastern part of London. He worked in the Trobriand Islands; some remote islands that belonged to the British Empire at that time. So he was not only interested in linguistics but in anthropology as well.

You find some of his books having 'insulting' titles like 'The Sexual Life of the Savages'. Anyway Malinowski, if we forget about his prejudices and talk about his purely linguistic contributions, especially semantics, we find that he would link language to culture. Each language is closely linked to its particular culture. You cannot understand its meaning unless you put it back in its context. And the term CONTEXT is very important not only for him but for all the members of the London School.

Another semantic concept found with Malinowski is that the meaning of a sentence could be equated with the observable results achieved by uttering it. For instance, 'stand up!' equals the act: 'THE STUDENTS STAND UP'. 'Look out of the window!' equals the act: 'THE STUDENT LOOKS OUT OF THE WINDOW.' It is called PERFORMATIVE. When a prisoner is executed, one should not look at the hangman and say that the hangman is responsible for killing him or look at the rope! These are just means. They are tools. The one who really killed the prisoner is the sentence: *I sentence you to death*, uttered by the judge. So according to Malinowski as well as for philosophers like Wittgenstein, Austin, Quine, Searl, etc., language is not to 'tell' but to 'do'. It is not 'telling'; it is 'doing'.

MICHAEL HALLIDAY (-d 2018) was one of the founding members of this school. Nowadays, many people are working within his frame; especially in teaching and translation. Many students are writing their PhDs in linguistics and translation at different world universities, following his approach to syntax. He has a book called *Syntax and the Consumer*. Notice the phrase 'the consumer'; a sentence is not just a syntactic structure. So like the rest of the members of London, Halliday takes into consideration the 'use of language'. Words are 'tools', when one looks at their shape, usually one asks the question 'what for is this?' He looks for the possible 'use' of that tool. Now a tool could be just a screwdriver which needs only one person to use it or, a boat or a plane in which case you need a whole crew.

Halliday looks at syntax through three dimensions: SYSTEM, RANK and DELICACY (the – scale). SYSTEM is a term to remember, as it applies to the whole approach of this school. It simply means a set of possibilities (exclusive alternatives), choices or as the teachers of English would call it a 'table of substitution.'

So, for instance in a sentence like *Mary came home late yesterday*, we can substitute: she/our neighbour/the person living next door, etc. for: *Mary*. Those possibilities will be put one above the other between BRACES; so the braces are not just a notation, hanging around. It is actually a theoretical representation. They represent a certain syntactic relation. They are different from the parentheses and the square brackets. Each representation has its own meaning.

Another London School term is RANK. It can be illustrated by an example from chemistry. The smallest unit in nature is the atom, a few atoms make a molecule, billions of molecules make a cell, Millions of cells make an organ and finally the organs make up an organism, i. e. a body [the biologist may correct me!]. To take an illustration from sociology, you could say that the individual is the smallest (hopefully indivisible unit), at least two individuals make up a family; the children, optional (?). Families make a tribe, especially in the country-side. Hundreds of tribes make up a nation and the nations of the world make up humanity.

In syntax, Halliday suggests something similar. Each rank is included in a bigger rank. He suggests 5 ranks for English: MORPH, WORD, GROUP, CLAUSE and finally SENTENCE. So, for instance, in a sentence like: *Any gangster trying to ride the stallion will be thrown off*. You have *gangster* which starts with the morph *gang*. The morph *gang* is the first rank. It is included in the second rank which is the word *gangster*. In its turn, gangster is included in the third rank which is the group: *any gangster* (called phrase by other linguists like Chomsky). The group *any gangster* is included in the one but last group: *any gangster trying to ride the stallion* and finally this clause is included in the largest rank which is the sentence: *Any gangster trying to ride the stallion will be thrown off.*

Finally, Halliday suggests DELICACY which means that, if I said: "Well, look at this picture [Maggie Thatcher]." Suppose I asked you this question: "what's the difference between her and a human being?" You would be astonished. What's the difference between these two words, PERSON and THATCHER? The difference is that one is included in the other. 'Person' is more inclusive than 'Thatcher' and the latter is more precise than the former 'person.' 'Person' includes millions of other entities besides Thatcher; whereas Mrs. Thatcher is just one person i.e. the former 'Iron Lady' of England.

Actually, in here we have a scale of delicacy. In our case, the scale (or hierarchy) would go: PERSON/WOMAN/ENGLISH WOMAN/ENGLISH WOMAN DOING POLITICS/THATCHER. One item is less inclusive than the preceding one, but at the same time more precise. The higher we go in the scale of delicacy the less referents there are and the more precise our term becomes.

This is especially relevant for translation; take the example of a student who translated 'خْضَرَ' (Moroccan Arabic) as 'not boiled' (cf. raw). He has gone too high in the scale of delicacy. Because this scale presents us with: 'not cooked' and 'not boiled' (together with other equally possible interpretations like 'not roasted', i.e. cooked with no oil, no water and no coal!).

To go back to the consumer. If you hear from someone this sentence: *I have a vehicle*, you can guess that he has chosen the lowest item of the scale; can you guess the kind of vehicle? He has probably just a bicycle. Because if he had a Rolce Royce or a Juguar he would go to the highest point in the scale:

    Jaguar-English Car-Car-Vehicle

To sum up, the London School is also referred to as SYSTEMIC LINGUISTICS (pronounced /sisti:mik/). It could rightly be referred to as SYSTEMIC AND CONTEXTUAL. Because each context requires one (and only one) item from a given system.

This approach, consisting of SYSTEM and CONTEXT, is applied by the London scholars to all linguistic levels, namely PHONOLOGY, SYNTAX, and SEMANTICS.

First, in phonology we could consider examples of STRESS and ASSIMILATION from English and Arabic. Take, for instance, *Mary came home late yesterday*. Suppose that this is what you knew and suppose that someone said that it was **John** who came late yesterday, what would you do? You would protest and show it with much emphasis on Mary: **Mary** came home late yesterday. Suppose, he said that Mary went away, you would stress **came** home and likewise **late,** if he said early, and **yesterday** if he said two days ago. So we see that there is a SYSTEM of stress options. Each option applies to a given context (the context made by the words of the sentence or more broadly by the discussion.)

Now ASSIMILATION: suppose we had the following Arabic paradigm:

من عاد	n	q
من يئس	j →	j
من كان	n	k
من تاب	n	t

We noticed that for each context corresponds one item from the system n/j/n/n (Dental).

Sometimes to refer to the vertical relationship by PARADIGMATIC and SYNTAGMATIC as the horizontal one is misleading. This could be remedied perhaps by considering PARADIGM as EITHER OR relation, and SYNTAGM as AND relation. So, in English ASSIMILATION also works by SYSTEM and CONTEXT. Take for instance *human being*, /n/ becomes /m/ in the environment of /b/ which give:

'human being' → /huma-*m*-being/

In SYNTAX, the same approach is used that is the SYSTEM/CONTEXT dimensions. Take for instance, the sentence *Mary came home late yesterday*, to pick that one again. It is a syntactic context and allows for 4 systems, at least. [see Ben Rochd *Words* 2020d]

In semantics, according to Malinowsky, you cannot interpret the meaning of a sentence without its context. And this bears heavily on TRANSLATION and TEACHING. You cannot translate a text without its context. And you cannot teach a foreign language without its context. As an alternative of sending the learner to England which is the proper context of English, some teachers suggest the alternative of the classroom. And this reminds me of my first experience in teaching. I was given to the supervision of a teacher of English for beginners. He was short and dynamic. He was asking his pupils the question 'what is the teacher doing? and doing the action. They would answer, 'he is running', 'he is jumping', he is ..., etc. He was very dynamic. I thought to myself I would never be able to do this! I can just say it!

As a CONCLUSION: Go to England if you want to do PHONETICS and 'do it!' Good luck!

3. ROBERT LE PAGE

Robert Le Page is a famous linguist thanks to his contributions:

1.   "ACTS of IDENTITY" which deals with the sociolinguistic problems faced by black minorities in white 'supremacist' societies (like the case of Malcolm X).
2.   Computer Aided Cluster Analysis.
3.   The "Four Riders" or "Four Senses" as explained by Le Page himself:

"The Four senses are:

Sense One refers to what is felt to be a speaker's native language, or which he uses in his most informal and relaxed behaviour with his peers. William Labov has tried to capture language in this sense, claiming that linguists normally work as informants. I believe 'language' in this sense to be a purely hypothetical construct, a linguistic base – line which the individual needs, but without other justification and certainly inaccessible. Peer-group behaviour is just as much conditioned by my hypothesis and its riders as solipsist behaviour or lame behaviour, the 'me' who is talking to my wife is no more the 'real me' than the 'me' talking to my students, although I certainly take up different roles and these roles have different linguistic symptoms.

Sense Two is what is accessible through performance. It is socially-marked behaviour. It reflects the groups which the individual believes exist in his society and his desire to be identified with or distinguished from them. This SOCIALLY-MARKED DATA is what forms the basis for the learner's creation of his linguistic systems; it is what the sociolinguist is learning to work with; the linguist and the psycholinguist have yet to recognize it for what it is.

Sense Three is the linguist's descriptive abstraction from the data. It is always partial, and always powerfully conditioned by the linguist's linguistic theories and educational experience. It tends to concentrate on those aspects of language which have traditionally been described —and we owe a good deal to Malinowski, to Firth and to Dell Hymes for helping to rescue us from that particular treadmill. Once the descriptions are made, two things happen: 'the language' becomes for many purposes particularly within the educational system – that

WHICH HAS BEEN DESCRIBED, so that when we learn e.g. French it is this artefact, the phonology grammar lexicon of it, which we are asked to learn, and in which we are examined. Secondly, it becomes inevitably prescriptive, and provides a powerful focusing agent for the behaviour of educated groups, so that many communities becomes bilingual or diglossic by virtue of their members needing to show that they are familiar with a particular artefact of an elite in their society. (See De Silve, 1976, 1979).

Sense Four is very similar to Saussure's langue. It is inherent in the daily behaviour of a community as well as in its oral or written memory, laws, stereotypes. It can never be fully described, and is, of course, continually changing. Partial abstractions made from time are not always comparable, since they may draw on different members of the community or different modes of behaviour or be cast in different moulds, though it is these partial abstractions which usually constitute the basis of comparative and historical linguistics. There is theoretical continuity of transmission of linguistic models either geographically or historically from community to community or from generation to generation or both, but we are not in a position to make a complete inventory of sense four language for any community and the narrow genetic metaphor is more misleading than helpful. I believe that Bickerton's Dynamic of a Creole system '1975' is an attempt to describe a language - 'The Guyanese Language'- in sense four, and is extremely valuable for that reason alone even though the attempt revealed —as I feel it was bound to- the impossibility of the task. Dell Hymes similarly has set linguists an impossible task in calling for descriptions of communicative competence. It is much more complex than describing how to use money; and the latter task has so far defeated economists.

15. MARRISM

Marrism is the linguistic theory of the Soviet Union before 1950. It drew on Marxist dichotomy and dialectics of "super-structure" being determined by "infra-structure".

According to Robins (R.H. 1967): "Marr, himself a Georgian by birth and from his early youth gifted with remarkable language learning ability, turned his attention first, like some other Russian scholars, to Georgian and the rest of the Caucasian languages. In investigating the history of the Caucasian languages he gradually evolved his own theory (or theories) of linguistic history. Rejecting the accepted Indo-European theory, he drew his ideas from eighteenth-century beliefs in the gestural origin of language and from middle nineteenth-century opinion on linguistic typology as an indication of stages of progressive linguistic development. The 'Japhetic' languages, a term he used to cover the languages of the Caucasus, represented a stage in the evolution of language through which some other languages had already passed. Languages were historically related, not in linguistic families, but by the different evolutionary 'layers' of structure deposited from continual mixtures and combinations. Languages were not national, but class phenomena, and were part of the superstructure whose changes correspond in the economic base of the speakers' social organization; here he claimed the theoretical alliance of Marrism and Marxism.

Claiming to explain not only linguistic history but also linguistic prehistory by his theory, Marr soon transcended mere observational statements, and declared that the words of all languages could be traced back to four primitive elements: [sal], [ber], [jon] and [rosh]. Such unsupported theorizing enjoyed official patronage, and several other Russian scholars found it prudent to uphold and even eulogize Marr's pronouncements, until 1950 when suddenly Stalin ordained the rejection of the whole Marrist edifice, pointing out, among other things, that language was not dependent on economic organization since the same Russian language served both pre-revolutionary capitalism and post-revolutionary communism, a statement of the obvious not apparently made before. Stalin's intervention both ended the long reign of Marrist theory and drew the world's attention to it."

The Russian of the 'comrades' was the same as the one of the **Tsar**!!

16. WITTGENSTEIN

Ludwig Wittgenstein was one of the philosophers of Cambridge. Although from Austrian origin, he worked and lived in England, and was one of the positivist (empiricist) philosophers like August Comte and Francis Bacon, and more specifically one of the ordinary-language philosophers like Austin and Quine.

He criticized philosophy bitterly as it has according to him wasted too much time on pseudo-problems. Whereas its first task and aim should be to investigate LANGUAGE.

Wittgenstein is considered as one of the best (Anglo-Saxon) philosophers of the twentieth century, who wrote extensively about language and religion. We may rightly ask, 'what are the new things that brought up this philosopher in these two fields of knowledge?'

It is worth bearing in mind that the religion of Wittgenstein's parents was Christianity. His family was wealthy but Wittgenstein himself was not interested in money and preferred to live simply. For him there are no philosophical problems, but just linguistic confusion. Yet, he had a long life interest in religion and claimed to see every problem from a religious point of view. However, he said in his 1992 *Lecture on Ethics*, that the tendency of all men who ever tried to write about ethics or religion was to run against the boundaries of language. This gave support to the view that Wittgenstein believed in mystical truth that somehow cannot be expressed meaningfully but is of the utmost importance.

Not surprisingly, Wittgenstein wants the reader of his books not to think so much but to look at the language **game** that gives rise to philosophical problems. Obviously, in a world of contingency one cannot prove that a particular attitude is the correct one to take. Thus, the spirit of relativism seems far from Wittgenstein's conversation and absolute tolerance. With regard to religion this philosopher is often considered a kind of anti-realist, who emphasized doctrine or philosophical arguments intended to prove God's existence, but was greatly drawn to religious rituals and symbols. He had even considered becoming a priest once.

Wittgenstein's way of using the word 'GRAMMAR' is a key to understanding his work in philosophy, he said that, 'any explanation of the use of language was grammar,' which includes whatever is needed to describe the meaning of language. For instance, the part of speech 'noun' is defined as the name of a person, place, or thing. Still, Wittgenstein called into question our textbook definitions. To ask for example whether by calling all nouns names of objects, emotions, numbers and so on, we do not cover up profound differences in the ways we use words. And so to ask whether school grammar, and the inferences we draw from it, may lead us to misunderstand the logic of language. If we classify any particular word as a noun, we have already gone some way towards giving the word its meaning. Therefore according to Wittgenstein, by grammar, we shall mean the rules of using a sign and also the account we give of those rules.

According to Jasper Doomen [p.c.], it is important to know that most interpreters of Wittgenstein's work distinguish two periods: in the first period, he develops a philosophy according to which language mirrors the world: a situation corresponds to a description in words. A famous example is this: Wittgenstein read about a court trial in the newspaper. In this trial, a model car was used to represent the real car. In the same way, a picture consists of elements, each of which stands in a relation of correspondence or reference to some object. This is his famous picture theory.

The book in which he expounds his ideas is *Tractatus Logico-Philosophicus*, a short work with a great number of theses and subtheses. Thesis 2.1 (p.14) runs as follows: "We construe pictures of the facts." Furthermore, "the picture is a model of reality." (thesis 2.12 (p.15)). The picture is a standard of reality (according to thesis 2.1512 (p.15)). "A sentence can only be true or false insofar as it is a picture of reality" (thesis 4.06 (page 30)); "The sentence is a picture of reality" (thesis 4.01 (page 26)).

He appeals to a sort of **logical atomism** (the philosopher Bertrand Russell defended a philosophy with this name): the smallest parts of language, the atoms, serve as the bases for sentences: "The simplest sentence, the elementary sentence ('Elementarsatz' in German), asserts the being of a state of affairs." (thesis 4.21(page 38)).

He initially thought to have solved all philosophical queries and abandoned philosophy. But in time, he concluded that language is too complex to be merely characterized as the simple linguistic reconstruction of the world. His most important work written after *Tractatus Logico-Philosophicus* is a work called *Philosophische Uuntersuchungen* (Philosophical Investigations), published after his death. This is representative of the second period.

In this book, he is critical of his earlier views. He represents the following example: suppose one is dealing with the sentence 'five red apples'. According to his earlier views, there should be a correspondence between the atomic facts and the world (his earlier view; cf. thesis 4.21 of the *Tractatus Logico-Philosophicus mentioned above*), but he now casts doubt on this view by asking what exactly the five refers to (page 238). It cannot, after all, be pointed out. The same problem comes to the fore when one wants to make it clear that something is not red; to what does one, then refer? Obviously not to something red (page 415)).

Instead of maintaining, as he did in the *Tractatus Logico-Philosophicus*, that **language** as such corresponds to **things**, he differentiates between various language games, 'Sprachspiele' in German (page 241). The language game is an activity, or a form of life (page 250). Rules constitute an important part of this exposition (pages 270, 271). In this approach, it is '**use,**' which determines the meaning of sentences. If one should, for example, want to clarify what a game is, examples are presented. It is not of importance to see a general characteristic in these, but to use them (page 280).

So Wittgenstein's main idea must be answered twofouldly. His main idea in the first period is that one gives an analysis of the world through language; there is a clear correlation between the way the world is constituted and its representation through language. One should not say anything which cannot be said (thesis 6.53 (page 85)). By the way: Wittgenstein states himself, 'It is my main thought, that the "logical constants" can't be substituted. That the logic of facts can't be substituted.' The original German runs as follows: "Mein Grundgedanke ist dab die" logischen Konstanten' nicht vertreten. Dab sich die Logik der Ttsachen nicht vertreten labt. (thesis 4.0312(page 29)). He sees the purpose of philosophy in clarifying thoughts logically (thesis 4.112 (page 33)).

His main idea in the second period is that there is no common standard for making sense of the world (as he had thought himself in the *Tractatus Logico-Philosophicus*), but that language games are decisive for individual situations and that the application of language is primary.

This approach must be followed in answering the question: what Wittgenstein's opinion about religion is, as well. His opinion about religion in the first period is relatively easy stated: religion cannot, according to him, be expressed using language. That is, he does not express atheism, but the subject cannot be dealt with within the limits language poses, 'How the world is, is completely indifferent for the Higher being. God does not present himself in the world." (thesis 6.432

(page 84)). It is important to know what Wittgenstein means by 'the world': the world is everything which is the case; it is the completeness of facts, not of things. (theses 1 and 1.1 (page 11))

The mystical can't be expressed; it shows itself (thesis 6.522 (page 85)). He concludes the *Tractatus Logico-Philosophicus* with the famous phrase 'Woveon man nicht sprechen kann, daruber mub man schweigen.' (**"Whereof one cannot speak, one must be silent"**) (thesis 7 (page 85)). In the Philosophische Untersuchungen, his position is not clearly conveyed.

Wittgenstein was a student of Russell's who had suggested the sentence "the King of France is bald" in a famous and influential article, meaning that: there is one and only one entity that is the King of France and that entity is bald" (thus false, because there is no such entity. In contrast, "The Queen of England is visiting Morocco" would be true or false depending on whether that entity, which does exist, in fact has the property "visiting Morocco." (Chomsky, p.c.)

Bertrand Russell was proud of his student WITTGENSTEIN. He used to say "soon he knew all I had to teach" and called him "Mr. Wittgenstein".

Some of the technical terms used by Wittgenstein among other logicians are synthetic vs. analytic truth, excluded middle, middle term, sophistry, logical connectives. Let us exemplify them in turn.

TRUTH can be either Synthetic, i.e. observable, or Analytic, depending on reason alone. EXCLUDED MIDDLE is a case of reasoning where you have only two options; nothing in between e.g. All roses are either yellow or red. MIDDLE TERM is the predicate of the major premise and the subject of the minor premise. It is what you delete to obtain the conclusion of the syllogism, e.g. All men are mortal – Socrates is a man – Socrates is mortal.

SOPHISTRY is a seemingly sound deduction but is not such as: All cats eat fish – John eats fish - John is a cat.

Dealing with the Logical CONNECTIVES such as 'then' (implication) Wittgenstein establishes the following Truth Table

It rains	It's wet	→ If it is raining (then) it will be wet
1	1	1
1	0	0
0	1	1
0	0	1

17. BLOOMFIELDIANS

One can hardly imagine American structuralism without thinking about "**Sapir-Whorf hypothesis**" (cf. Wittgenstein). It is the hypothesis that: "language creates thought." Man does not live in the real physical world but rather in a "linguistic world." Every people have their own special world which goes hand in hand with the structure of their language. It is Language that shapes their sensibility of life, in one way or another. As an example, you may translate the sentence "La France a élu son président" into English by using a neutral pronoun "France has elected its president." in Arabic by using the feminine pronoun (-ha), not to forget that the source language i.e. French, uses a masculine possessive pronoun "son."

This poses the problem of translation. You may try to translate the word "Hamburger" in Arabic (?) It further poses the problem of the reality of things in the real world and their equivalents in language. *Coal* for instance seems to be a simple substance, whereas *diamond* is so attractive and expensive. Still the chemist will tell you that they are both representations of the same chemical element.

Sapir-Whorf hypothesis stems from real experiences lived by the two men. As a fireman, Whorf witnessed that people were caress besides so-called "empty petrol drums" while they were very cautious besides "full petrol drums." This behaviour led many times to the breaking of fires, as the "empty petrol drums" are more dangerous that the full petrol drums. They contain explosive gases. So Whorf noticed that people live in a linguistic world rather than the real one, as the two words "empty" and "full" played a crucial role in determining their behaviour.

Sapir also noted the same phenomenon in the behaviour of Indian speakers of Hopi. These people could not fit in the modern life as they were unable to conceive the time sections. Their language lacks the time portions. Other Indian tribes can count only up to 4: 1, 2, 3, 4, 4, 4…anything above 3 is 4 even if it is a 1.000. 000.

Sapir-Whorf hypothesis can be summed up into 2 principles: "Relativism" and "determinism." The first one means that people's ideas and languages differed indefinitely (by opposition to Universalists). The second principle means that the individual is not free in his conception of the world, not even in his linguistic behaviour (by opposition to Robert le Page's Acts of Identity). He is a "linguistic prisoner" (no Alcatraz escape!). His mind is moulded by the language he is using.

Semantic studies did not draw enough attention from the American structuralists as it is a "vague domain", except for a few, such as *colors* and *kinship*. You can divide the rainbow into 7 colors, or 6, or even 3: red, yellow and blue. The other colors can be obtained from the combination of those 3. Orange is the combination of red and yellow, green is the combination of yellow and blue. In fact you could reduce the colors to just one: "white."

Human languages divide the light spectrum into different categories. Some languages give the same name to two colors (cf. Berber *aziza*), some give to *blue* two names, one for clear and one for dark. But all those names do not coincide by any means with reality as described by physicists. They claim that there are 7.500.000 colors... amazing! This is another proof that language is relative on the one hand and that each language creates its own thought. If we suppose the existence of a language that has only 3 words for the description of colors, its speakers will be forced to talk about 3 colors only? The same thing applies to "snow" considered as one single substance, while the Eskimo has many words to describe different genres of snow. Similarly, the aboriginal Australians (or ancient Arabs) have different words to describe different genres of 'sand'.

The American structuralists are usually referred to as "Descriptivists and taxonomists" and sometimes as "Discovery procedure linguists." The most popular of whom is Leonard Bloomfield, but in fact "American Saussure" is Franz Boas, who was the pioneer of this school. Structuralism appeared simultaneously on both sides of the Atlantic Ocean. In his book *Handbook of American Indian Language*, Boas had no choice, but the synchronic approach, as he knew next to nothing about the history of the languages of the Native Americans. Boas and his co-workers faced the problems of a new type of data, as the Indian languages differed totally from the Indo-European languages.

FRANZ BOAS (1858-1942)

Franz Boas was a German-born American linguist and anthropologist of the nineteenth and beginning of the twentieth centuries. A pioneer of the filed, basing his theory on 'RELATIVISM and DETERMINISM" as will be dubbed the "Sapir-Whorf" hypothesis (vs Chomsky's UG). He worked as a professor at Columbia University and was the founder of the first anthropology Dept in the US. He is also a specialist of Native American languages and cultures, besides been a teacher of a number of scientists. (see his notorious book *Handbook of American Indian Language*).

LEONARD BLOOMFIELD (1887-1949)

Bloomfield is an American linguist born in Chicago (1887). He is considered to be the head of American structuralism. For him language consists of phonemes (its smallest units), which combine to make morphemes (bound and free), and finally phrases and sentences. His approach to language is closely related to behaviourist psychology (see the Story of Jack and Jill) (see his important book *Language* 1933)

He is the major figure of descriptive (distributional) Linguistics in North America of the 20th century and leading figure of all subsequent research. He was first educated at Harvard, Wisconsin and Chicago universities. He later became lecturer at many universities and professor of Germanic philology and comparative Linguistics at the Universities of Chicago and Yale.

He was first concerned with the Indo-European language family especially, its peculiar phonology and word formation. Then he enlarged his scope from Germanic languages to exotic languages such as Malayo-Polynesian amongst others. This new direction of his research can be found in his book *An Introduction to the Study of Language* (1914). Then, in the early 20's of last century, he turned his attention to North American Indian languages. It was a huge comparative, descriptive and innovative work on non-European language family.

His linguistic approach was selective and reductive in the sense that he believed that language can be studied in abstraction from its environment in a purely scientific way. He still based it on the behaviouristic psychology of Watson, as can be seen in his most famous book *Language (1933)*. (see the story of **Jack and Jill** and **car-mody anecdote**). His approach to language was purely empirical. (see *A Leonard Bloomfield Anthology* (1970) was edited by Charles F. Hackett.)

Avoiding 'Euro (West)-centrism, he recognized on several occasions, that he was making use of concepts and techniques that were to be found in Panini's work on Sanskrit, produced some two and a half millennia ago." (Koerner and Asher 1995). Bloomfield further described Panini's work as a "monument of intelligence."

Bloomfield remains the most outstanding person of this linguistic trend though. He, together with Charles Hockett, are responsible for establishing the concepts of the "phoneme" (compare with Trubetzkoy and Sweet) in phonology. They are also responsible for the concepts of "ITEM AND ARRANGEMENT" on the one hand and "ITEM AND PROCESS" on the other. Add to these the notion of "PORTMANTEAU", and "IMMEDIATE CONSTITUENT ANALYSIS" in syntax. As an example of item and arrangement consider the Arabic word *kitaban*. This word consists of two morphemes *kitab+an*. While item and process would say for a word such *kutub* is a transformation from *Kitab* to *kutub* (*malik* → *malikun* in Palmer 1984). The portmanteau approach would say that one morpheme is related to two morphemes such as *seek* to *sought*, which carries the verb "seek" plus PAST, vs. follow → flowed. Immediate Constituent Analysis divides the sentence into its major elements starting from the biggest units until it reaches its smallest undividable element i.e. the morpheme. (Palmer 1984) Take the example of the sentence: *the man was advised to eat honey*. It can be divided into the following morphemes:

[the-man-was-advis-ed-to-eat-honey]

According to Drimmer, the author of *Black History*, the white man's 'Indian genocide' feeling of guilt, was among the motives that pushed some American scholars to study the structure of the Indian languages before their extinction. It is believed that the Indians were swept away by 90 °/°. (In the 60s, AIM movement once stated that the Indians are more numerous than when Christopher Columbus discovered America. Still, they are now shown as a mere touristic attraction. They are kept secluded in reservations; modern slavery?).

EDWARD SAPIR (1884-1939)

Sapir Edward was an American linguist, from German origin, and one of the founders of phonology and typology. (See *Language an Introduction to the Study of Speech* (1921). Sapir's name is usually linked to Whorf's name in what is known as the Sapir-Whorf hypothesis.

The Sapir-Whorf position could be reduced to two principles: RELATIVISM and DETERMINISM. By the first one it is meant that people's perceptions of the world as well as the structure of their languages are endlessly diverse. There is no universality. As far as the second principle is concerned, it means that the individual does not choose his world view or even his behaviour, he rather finds himself caught up, so to speak, in a linguistic prison from which there is no possible escape. His mind is moulded by the structure of the language he uses.

BENJALIN LEE WHORF (1897-1914)

American linguist, a student of Sapir. He developed the connection between language and cognition, based on Hebrew and other languages. This equation became known as the Sapir-Whorf hypothesis. The structure of a given language conditions the way of thinking of its speakers. Languages differ indefinitely and hence differences of thinking and culture, and how the people view reality and the world. (See German Humboldt). Applying this theory (language/ideas) to non-European languages, the duo noticed important differences. Native Americans viewed time and punctuality as they are dictated by the grammar (especially verb tenses) of their respective languages.

KENNNETH PIKE (1912-2000)

There was another innovative structuralist trend in America led by Kenneth Pike. It is known as Tagmemic Linguistics. Its primary goal is MISSIONARY WORK. It aims at converting the tribes of central and South America to Christianity. It is based at the Summer Institute of Linguistics (SIL). It has realized so far a big deal, and only a few thousand languages remain to be dealt with, so as to transmit the Holy Book to everyman in his own mother tongue! (Sampson 1980).

According to Pike an *emic* unit is 'an entity seen as "same" from the perspective of the internal logic of the containing system, as if it were unchanging even when the outside analyst easily perceives the change' (xii). An *etic* unit is 'the point of view of the outsider as he tries to penetrate a system alien to him; and it also labels some component of an emic unit, or some variant of it, or some preliminary guess at the presence of internal emic units, as seen either by the alien observer or as seen by the internal observer when somehow he becomes explicitly aware of such variants through teaching or techniques provided by outsiders.

Kenneth Pike is against restricted approaches to linguistics and chooses to start in linguistic analysis from *social interaction* which opens perspectives for studying dialogue, sentence, pronunciation, differences between people in particular and various contexts (xiii).

Tagmemic theory is complex, because it requires considering context 'at every step: that is, in all perception and experience and knowledge' (xiv). This theory is synonymous to *unit-in-context* (xiv). We may approach things that have some kind of relationship in so many different ways, and while trying to determine the nature of the relationships between them, we tend to look for what is useful, but 'so often, [we are obliged to do so] on the form in which (…) facts are given' (xiv).

Pike wants his theory to be suitable to as many fields and situations as possible and not only to linguistics. 'HUMAN EMIC experience is the target, not merely linguistics' (xv), he states.

The **Tagmemic** theory came as a result of so many researches and attempts to find as general principles as possible (that would be applicable to a wide range of languages). The theory revealed itself to be even applicable to other fields of research (anthropology for ex.)

Finally, **ZELLIG HARRIS (1909-1992)**, who is considered as the culmination of American structuralism in the first half of the 20th c. He is the one who paved the way to what was going to be a revolution in modern Linguistics at the hands of his brilliant student Noam Chomsky.

18. CHOMSKY

Chomsky's Minimalist Program
and Arabic Non-Concatenation

[*In remembrance of late Khalid Touzani*]

[For the evolution of Chomsky's TG grammar, since its earliest insemination, see Ben Rochd *Evolution of Chomsky's TG Grammar, 2020a*]

INTRODUCTION

'If we are satisfied that an apple falls to the ground because that is its natural place, there will be no serious science of mechanics. The same is true if one is satisfied with traditional rules for forming questions, or with the lexical entries in the most elaborate dictionaries, none of which come close to describing simple properties of these linguistic objects.' (Chomsky 1997)

1. PHILOSOPHY

The minimalist program is concerned with the place of language in the human mind/brain. So, it is a cognitive theory of language. It tries to answer the psychological question of language learnability: why is it possible for the child to learn language but not for any other biological creature? It even tries to answer the philosophical question about man's uniqueness in the organic world? 'Language seems to be unique among the Cognitive Systems (=acquiring knowledge), and man seems to be unique in the organic world!

Sure enough, there are tensions and conflicts between observational, descriptive and explanatory theories of language, respectively those that state which sequences of sounds are (un)acceptable in a given language (1a) Those that state that plus describe the structure of the sequence as in (1b). Finally, those that presumably provide explanatory principles for language acquisition (1c):

(1)

a. *geek (vs. Beautiful)

b. [S[NP The Linguist] [VP saw [NP the squirrel]] [PP in High-Gate cemetery]

c. X-bar/Minimalist Program/ Kayne's LCA

2. MINIMALIST MODEL

Since the early '60s the central objective of generative grammar was to abstract principles from the complex rule systems advised for particular languages, leaving rules that are simple maximally constrained. So instead of passive, question, dative, etc. we have a simple rule called move alpha which is part of the computational system. Consider (2):

(2)

a. The ball was hit   t

b. man jaaʔa   t

"who come"

c. sa-ja-qraʔ-u-haa

"he will read it"

d. ʔal-BaTTatu llatii ʔakal-naa-haa

"the duck we ate"

In (2a) I moves to C. in (2b), there is a movement of the interrogative *man* to C. in (2c) the whole complex [TNS AGR V] is attracted initially.

According to Chomsky's Minimalist Program, the investigation in the language faculty should lead from the grammars of particular languages to the theory of languages and expressions they generate ie. Universal grammar (UG, for short).

UG aims at fixing the idealized model for language acquisition which is initial state S... or primary linguistic data (PLD for short). The interface level, provides instructions for the articulatory-perceptual and conceptual-intensional systems respectively. Each language will determine a set of pairs (a,b) draw from the A-P (PF) and C-I (LF) levels:

(3)

        (a PF] [LF b)

Linguistic variation will be found at PF and the lexicon, although Saussure had overlooked syntax which was excluded from *langue*. For him the structure of language was left to individual speakers who put words together on particular occasions. Chomsky's approach to this question was rather neat; it was that of a mathematician.

The computational system will take items form the lexicon and modify them. It will consist of X-bar and Move Alpha. The concepts of X-bar theory are therefore fundamental in a minimalist theory. In X-bar the head-complement relation is crucial as it is 'more local' than head specifier. It is also associated with theta-relations and Case. Move Alpha is constrained by Greed and Procrastinate. The basic structure of the sentence is taken to be (4):

(4)

[CP...   AGRS...TP...AGRO...VP]

[ibid]

There are two heads in this new sentence configuration: AGR-subject and AGR-object. Both consist of a collection of NP-features (gender, number, person). T will first raise to AGRS, forming (5b), and V raise to AGRo, forming (5b). The latter includes the NP-features of AGR and the Case feature provided by T, V. They are respectively illustrated in (5) and (6):

(5)

a. [AGRs T AGR]

b. [AGRo V AGR]

(6)

a. [AGRs sa-ja]

　　future-3sm

b. [AGRo qra?u-haa]

　　read-3sfACC

　"he (will) read it"

Notice that there is asymmetry between the subject and the object as far as their inflectional systems are concerned. On the other hand AGR can be 'active', 'inert' or missing.

In the early 80s Chomsky shifted his attention from a system of rules to a system of principles including case and government. The best example for these being classical Arabic. "John McCarthy has pointed out that classical Arabic has a lexical Case to the first NP following the verb and objective Case to the NP following it, leading to such sentences as (6):

(6)

(i) qatala zaydun alwaladan ("killed-active Zeyd-nominative the-boy-objective" – "Zeyd killed the boy")
(ii) qutila zaydun ("killed-passive Zeyd-nominative" – "Zeyd was killed")
(iii) Sirtu yawma ljumuʔati ("trazvelled-active-I Friday-objective" – "I travelled on Friday")
(iv) Sira yawmu ljumuʔati("trazvelled-passivefriday-nominative" – "Friday was travelled)"
(Chomsky 1980, p. 120)[poor IPA]

THE GUIDELINES OF THE MINIMALIST PROGRAM (1997)

(7)

a. A linguistic expression is a pair (a,b) generated by a minimal derivation satisfying interface conditions

b. The interface levels are the only levels of linguistic representation

c. All conditions concern the interface

d. Derivations are driven by morphological properties (move alpha)

e. Economy is expressed in terms of Greed and Procrastinate

Chomsky's Greed

'Move raises A only if morphological properties of A itself would not otherwise be satisfied in the derivation'. (Chomsky 1997: 302)

The morphological properties are TNS, AGR, CASE, ASP etc. as in (8):

(8)

a. John will/-ed come

b. Kitaab Zaid-i-n

c. kitaabu Zaid-GEN

"Zaid's book"

d. Zaid kataba kitaab

"Zaid wrote a book"

3. LANGUAGE TYPOLOGY (SVO/VOS)

Considering the differences between SVP languages, like English and VSO languages like Irish, Chomsky (1992) assumes that, 'V has raised overtly to I (AGRs) in Irish, while S and O raise in the LF component to SPEC-AGRs and SPEC-AGRo, respectively. We have only one way to express these differences: in terms of the strength of the inflectional features. One possibility is that the NP-features of Tense is strong in English and week in Irish; hence NP must rise to SPEC-[IP] in English prior to SPELL-OUT or the derivation will not converge; the procrastinate principle bars such raising in Irish. The EPP, which requires that [SPEC-IP] be realized (perhaps an empty category), reduces to morphological property of Tenses: strong or weak NP-features. Note that the NP-feature of AGR is weak in English, or we would have overt object-shift. We are still keeping to the minimal assumption that AGRs and AGRo are collections of features, with no relevant subject-object distinction, hence no difference in strength of features. Note also that a language might allow both weak and strong inflection, hence weak and strong NP-features:

Arabic is a suggestive case, with SVO versus VSO correlating with the richness of visible verb-inflection.'

As far as the correlation between rich/weak Infl and word-order are concerned, we can establish table (9):

(9)

WEAK	STRONG	BOTH
SVO	SVO	WEAK
STRONG		
English	Irish	VSO
SVO		
		Arabic

(10)

a. Arabic requires initial glottal stop as in the definite article /ʔal/ rather than /al/ also Arabic has velar /X/ rather than uvular /x/.

b. SVO, VSO, OSV word-orders (respectively) are optional, perhaps stylistically motivated. When you say: ʔal-Xubza ʔaakulu, it means I will eat bread exclusively, whereas if I say ʔaakulu ʔal-Xubz, VSO, it means that I will eat bread and I am ready to eat anything else. None of these is ungrammatical, nor greed motivated.

4. TENSE OR ASPECT?

It is noted that in Semitic languages verbal roots consist of only consonant clusters which are mapped onto vocalic melodies that constitute independent functional morphemes/categories. Among these melodies is the one that conveys aspectual information and which I assume is base generated under a syntactically independent ASOP node. Consonantal roots and vocalic melodies just like the standard cases of affixes, need to be mapped onto a host category to form a complete word, and hence well-formed in the morphological sense. Assuming this analysis to be correct the only change that needs to be effected in the structure is to replace TNSP with ASPP'.

Arabic imposes a peculiar morphology. Each word consists of a root of three letters which expresses a general concept which is linked to an amazing network of sense relations such as gender, number, voice, aspect, etc. that are expressed by a set of melodies. These are actually linked to different valencies at LF. When combined the root and the melodies yield different words or assign different grammatical features to the same word as mentioned before.

5. NON-CONCATENATIVE MORPHOLOGY

(11)

WRITING

                k-t-b   ROOT

Ø-uu i-aa aa-i   MELODIES

maktuub   kitaab   kaatib

"destiny"   "book"   "writer"

(12) * qu-til-at

"she was killed"

(13)

a. she was asked

b. suʔilat

In (13) there is a concatenation of three successive words she, was and ask-ed, in English. There is no such thing in Arabic (12) where, starting from the right, we can consider the at suffix as the feminine marker 'she' but no further segmentation can hold.

'Passive morphology, once again, is not necessarily associated with movement and assumption of a new GF.'

4/10 AGREEMENT

(14) ʔar-rajulu l-kariim-u

a.

1. NOMINATIVE   1

2. ACCUSATIVE

3. OBLIQUE

b.

4. DEFINITE

5. INDEFINITE   2

c.

6. SINGULAR   3

7. DUAL

8. PLURAL

d.

9. FEMININE

10. MASCULINE   4

6. CHOMSKY'S GREED

In non-concatenative languages like Arabic word morphology consists essentially of a root of three letters which express AGR, gender, number, voice, ASP, etc. These are linked to different logical argument structures.

Chomsky (1981) states 'Passive morphology, once again, is not necessarily associated with movement and assumption of a new GF. Much the same will be true in languages in which intransitives can be passivized as in Arabic, German, or Hebrew:

(15) a. sira yamna ljuumuʔati

travelled – pass.on Friday

    b. es wurde getanzt

        it was danced

    c. dubar ba

'was spoken about her'

This is actually not true in Arabic passive, ergative, causative and reflexive constructions. There is indeed a reshuffling of the LF with each transformation.

PASSIVE

In passive, the form CaCaCa c-selects NP1 agent and nominative followed by NP2 theme and objective. When transformed it drops and shifts nominative to NP2.

7. PF IN ARABIC

'We expect languages to be very similar at the LF level, differing only as a reflex of properties at PF'. Each language has its own PF principles. Some of the specific parameters of Arabic phonology are as in (16):

(16)

a. (C*)   (V*)

b. #*CCC

c. #*VVVV

d. #*CC

e. #*V

f. #CVCVCVCV

(see Ben Rochd *Generative Grammar* 1994a)

8. LOGICAL FORM

The concept of LOGICAL FORM has two meanings. Within the philosophical tradition, the concept developed in opposition to "grammatical form." Thus, the grammatical form of the sentence "the King of France is bald" was taken to be, basically, the surface structure, but the logical form, Bertrand Russell suggested in a famous and influential article, would be something like: there is one and only one entity that is the King of France and that entity is bald" (thus false, because there is no such entity. In contrast, "the Queen of England is visiting Morocco" would be true or false depending on whether that entity, which does exist, in fact has the property "visiting Morocco." (Chomsky, personal communication)

Many attribute the advances in FORMAL LINGUISTICS to Chomsky.

It is the study of grammar, or the development of theories as to how language works and is organized. Formal linguistics compares grammars of different languages, and by identifying and studying the elements common among them, seeks to discover the most efficient way to describe language in general. The ultimate goal is "Universal Grammar" – the development of a theory to explain how the human brain processes language. Within formal linguistics, there are three main schools of thought: traditional, structural and transformational.

19. PHONOLOGY

The phoneme was the primary target of the American (Bloomfieldian) descriptivists. "Discovery procedures" were made, by all means, to decipher this meaningful 'atom' of language from the continuum stretch of sounds of alien (usually Native American) languages under study. 'For Chomsky, on the other hand, it might well be claimed that syntax is the heart of linguistic science.' (Sampson 1980) still, Chomsky states that phonology is more interesting to study as its conclusions are easier to reach than in syntax. His grammar defines or rather **'generates'** (in the mathematical jargon) well-formed sentences. His contribution to phonology was dubbed "generative phonology." It was in fact the creation of Morris Halle of MIT, himself a student of Jakobson.

Bloomfield, and many of his co-workers believed that the 'phoneme' is the ultimate indivisible unit in the building of language. This new approach is based on a UNIVERSAL SET OF FEATURES. Each phoneme is considered as a 'distinctive parameter bundle.' It has split the 'atom' as it were into its constituents called 'distinctive features', such as voice, obstruent, coronal, etc. as an example you would deal with the de-voicing of /d/ to yield /t/ in German word finals, e.g. [bad] which rendered as /bat/, Berlin become (→) /perlin/, as a class rather than separate units.

This 'item and process' approach would deal with the phonological alternations (transformations) affecting 'natural classes' of sounds rather than single ones. So, according to Chomsky, phonology must be dealt with in phonetic features rather than in unitary segments, as the Bloomfieldians previous did.

The set of DISTINCTIVE FEATURES includes pairs such as 'obstruent-sonorant.' The first refers to those sounds making some kind of barrier on the way of the airflow (stops, fricatives, affricates). The other includes vowels, semi-vowels, nasals. Each set forms a natural class to which the same process applies. So, the rule applies to all obstruents rather than to stops only.

[-syllabic][+nasal][+coronal]→[-syllabic][+nasal][-coronal]/__   [Syllabic][-nasal][-coronal]

(see Ben Rochd, Generative Grammar, ms, University of Washington University 1994).

This process does not concern stops in German final position only, but all obstruents, and probably can be generalized to achieve UG. Jakobson, Halle and Chomsky based their phonology on the information provided by this binary-distinctive features approach. Processes such as (de)voicing, labialization, pharyngealization, could be explained in those terms. "in any case, even if the acoustic or perceptual effect of labialization were similar or even identical to that of pharygealization, say, nevertheless a complete description of Arabic would have to state that speakers use the latter rather than the former articulation, and vice versa in a description of Twi." (Sampson 1980)

It is strange that generative phonology came as a revolution in the 60's. The American linguists were comparatively 'weak' in phonetics. The English invented **IPA** was ignored in the US for 50 years. American linguists were 'armchair linguists' "given that neatly delimited data-base, one juggles with alternative formulations of rules like a Sherlock Holmes in his armchair." (ibid)

Sampson (1980) concludes that "the truth is, of course, that "Scientists are fully as fallible and often irrational as other men (...) sometimes, they dig in their heels(!)"

20. LABOV

"The study of variables is one of the central tasks of any investigation of the dialects of American cities. Applying the statistical methods of modern sociology, linguists have worked out investigative procedures sharply different from those of traditional dialectology. The chief contributor has been William Labov, the pioneer of social dialectology in the U.S. The basic task is to determine the correlation between a group of linguistic variables—such as the different ways of pronouncing a certain vowel—and extralinguistic variables, such as education, social status, age, and race. For a reasonable degree of statistical reliability, one must record a great number of speakers. In general, several examples of the same variable must be elicited from each individual in order to examine the frequency and probability of its usage. Accordingly, the number of linguistic variables that can be examined is quite limited, in comparison with the number of dialectal features normally recorded by traditional fieldworkers in rural communities; in these situations, the investigator is often satisfied with one or two responses for each feature." (Encyclopedia Britannica)

"William Labov was born on December the fourth 1927 in Rutherford (New Jersey). He studied at Harvard in 1948 from which he got his BA and worked as an industrial chemist from 1949 to 1961 before turning to linguistics. For his Master thesis he completed a study of change in the dialect of Martha's Vineyard, which was presented before the linguistic society of America to great acclaim. Labov took his PhD at Columbia University in 1963. He taught at Columbia from 1964 to 1970 before becoming a professor of linguistics at the University of Pennsylvania in 1971, which has become the Mecca for the discipline, and became director of the University's linguistic laboratory in 1977. The methods he used to collect data for his study of the varieties of English spoken in New York City, published as *The Social Stratification of English in New York City* in 1966, have been influential in social dialectology."

Labov stresses the need for African American Vernacular English (AAVE) to be respected and given its right status as a recognized variety of English, with its own grammatical rules. Still, the (AAVE) speakers should also be encouraged to learn standard American English so as to achieve two goals: communication, and social promotion. His study seminars gained much fame, especially his gatherings of people to tell their own linguistic experiences.

With his Yiddish background (Hebrew-German dialect of Eastern Europe), William Labov was a first-hand witness of language change in time, place, social contexts and human attitudes. His 1963 Masters written about the sound change in Martha's Vineyard and later his PhD thesis on sociolinguistics strata in New York City (Harlem) was the starting point of modern linguistic variation theory. Labov's intent was to develop an empirical, rigorous, and universal (?) approach to language as it is actually used, in real context.

His sound change studies led to develop a UG in modern phonology with universal and language-specific constraints. As an example his study of the /t/d/ sounds variations and different auxiliary renderings have been used for the study of several (non-English) languages. His primary focus was on the vowel system of American English (NY et al.) It has had an immense impact on subsequent dialectology studies. His survey studies and modern technological techniques based on computer aided technology, culminated in the publication of his notorious work: *Atlas of North American English*.

Labov's gender and class-based models of language variation is the key to understand the prestige gained by his approach and theory. His works include *Language in Inner City, Studies in Black English Vernacular* (1972), *Sociolinguistic Patterns* (1972) and *The Atlas of North American English* (2006). In the late 1960's, he 'broke' with the hard psychological "armchair linguistics' of the Chomskian paradigm, to achieve an adequate field research in language. He was mainly concerned with so-called 'Black American English', using the speech of the clerks working in stores; how they pronounced or dropped certain sounds. Their speech idiosyncrasies usually reflected their social condition; their voicing of /t/, their retroflex /r/, auxiliaries, etc. This represented the birth of a new discipline known as 'Social Dialectology.' It was a scientific study of dialectology based on the speech of the black inhabitants of New York City.

William Labov noted the differences and similarities in English pronunciation. It is well known that English has a major split between Received Pronunciation (RP) and General American (GA). The latter is noted for its back vowels and /t/ voicing, as can be heard in American pronunciation of the dollar's motto "In God We Trust" and "New York City" (pronounced /gad/ and /sidi/) (Ben Rochd 2021).

In grammar black American English is well known for its (illogical) double negation e.g. *I ain't never done nothing*! and the dropping of present tense 3rd person suffix –s e.g. *he do it*. These features probably come from the south and due to the old slavery days, as in New Orleans, well -known for its 'soul food', 'soul music' and John Lee Hooker(?).

William Labov's Methods of socio-linguistic research can also remind us of English Robert Le Page's *Acts of Identity'* (1980) in his investigation of social variables: race, class, gender, age, education. Each linguistic variation in pronunciation or grammar corresponds to a specific regional dialect or social strata. Usually, Differences in speech determine people's group awareness and help the speaker in identifying, joining or rejecting, the visa-à-vis as potential 'friend or foe!'

Also, in any language, a special dialect is used as a means for social promotion as is testified in Bernard Shaw's play *Pygmalion*. For finding a job, the dress and the speech make up the success of the individual !

In England itself, you have differences in grammar and pronunciation, e.g. a couple discussing whether to use *cut* or *cutting* in "my nails need--" *poor* pronounced /pɔːr/ etc., to the extent that someone wondered: "Do the English speak English?" Not to forget Leonard Bloomfield's 'car-comedy theatre" anecdote!

"Sprachen machen Leute"

21. TRANSLATION

"From Roman times to the present, Europe has been a civilization of translations, every aspect of its culture, literature, administration, trade, religion, and science having been deeply influenced by translators. Modern thought on translation derives ultimately from the Jews of Alexandria in the first century BC who translated (the Bible) literally, and the Romans of the classical age, who did just the opposite. Two short passages have had an inordinate influence on translation theory: *De optimo genere oratorum* by Marcus Tullius Cicero (106-43 BC), which insisted on the necessity of 'weighing' words rather than 'counting them,' and the famous condemnation of literal translation by Horace (65-8) in his *Ars poetica* 131-35 (ca. 19 BC).» (LG Kelly 1995)

Notwithstanding the saying "traduttore traditore," all big civilizations stemmed from translation: the Chinese from India (Buddhism), the Japanese from China (Kanji), the Arabic from Greek (Aristotle), the French from Arabic ('Paris row' 13th c.'). Translation is sometimes seen a dangerous rival to the original (Pickthall). It is generally, motivated by religion, politics, administration, or simply, everyday communication (dialects of the same language). The art of 'TRANSLATION" seems to be universal, and follows its own chronology. Let's start from the beginnings...

1) BABYLON

Translation was a constant of ancient civilizations – there are bilingual inscriptions from Assyria and Mesopotamia (3000 BC) and the Rosetta stone from Egypt (196 BC). Most of these translations dealt with administrative and commercial matters.

2) FAR-EAST

China embraced Indian Buddhism. And, "With the spread of Buddhism to China came knowledge of some of the ancient Sanskrit *Sutras* (...) so the need to translate and transliterate the Sanskrit sutras led to the development of new ideas in China. The early introduction of the Chinese writing system (KANJI) and the introduction of Buddhism to Japan provided a certain stimulus.

3) MIDDLE EAST

After the Arab conquest of Iraq in 637, it became the haven of culture and civilization (similar to Andalusia). During the Abbasid rule, it knew its 'golden era' (8th c.) many intellectual achievements were realized. It stemmed from the translation of Greek classics, Plato's republic, Aristotle's categories.

"Amongst the most significant translation centres were the schools of the Muslim world at Baghdad, Seville, Toledo, and Cordova, where Greek philosophy and science were translated into Arabic."

"The thirteenth century controversy at the University of Paris over the translating of Greek philosophers from Arabic versions caused a fierce discussion. Roger Bacon, arguing from lexical and terminological evidence, condemned it out of hand (...), while other philosophers, notably Thomas Aquinas, speculated on the nature of translation, seeing it almost as a barter translation." (Kelly 1995)

4) JEWISH TRANSLATION

The Jewish translators of the Old Testament were based in Alexandria, which was one of the most important Greek-speaking cities of the Mediterranean. By 200 BC they were facing a dilemma. On the one hand most Jews living outside Palestine could not understand Hebrew well enough to read the scriptures. On the other, translation of the scriptures was tampering with the Word of God (...) the Greek version of the Hebrew Scriptures, the *Septuagint*, was complete by about 150 BC.. the persistent legend that the 70 translators were left in solitary confinement each with a Hebrew text and in 70 days each produced identical texts shows that literal translation was accorded mystical (dimension). [Try to translate "**until hell freezes**' into Arabic?]

5) THE MUSLIMS have the same attitude to the Word of God as Jews, translation of the Quran for religious purposes is suspect. In Europe, the Quran was translated early into European languages. These were 'curiosity-oriented' translations notably, into Latin dating from the 12th century. This was republished in 1543."

6) EUROPE

"The Christian translation of the Bible culminated in the work of St Jerome (348-420), famous for his Latin version of the Bible, the Vulgate (383-406)(...) In England there was a long progression from the Tyndale Bible of 1526-30 to the Authorized Version of 1611, which is an excellent example of teamwork. (King James Version)."

The sixteenth century, humanistic trend was essentially concerned with re-translations of the Bible, that was either for or against Reformation (Martin Luther's Bible (1534) is the most famous).

The European missionaries had their important part in Bible translations. During the 18th c., European expansion into the new world revived problems entailed in translating between sophisticated and unsophisticated languages. Little is known of how early Christian missionaries, like St Boniface (675-754), had faced the problems of creating literacy before being able to translate the Bible into languages previously unwritten."

7) The 17th c. Europe saw a somewhat shift from religion to philosophy. There was an enormous amount of translation of the European philosophers such as Bacon, Descartes', and, scientists such as English Isaac Newton's works." The goal of such endeavor was partly for education and partly for politics. The translation of history books served much in giving the regimes their 'legitimacy' as was done by fierce English Oliver Cromwell in Britain (1650).

8) After **World War II**, translation followed other trends, to solve urgent needs, in politics and commerce.

9) THEORIES

Translation is based on the well-known trilogy of 'source language- target language-translator".' This must be an almost impossible task, if we believe the Sapir Whorf relativistic theory.

In England John Dryden suggested his translation typology: 'metaphrase,' 'paraphrase' and 'imitation.' Most famous German poet by J.W. Goethe (1749-1832) gave his own classification: literal, 'parody.' Goethe's ideas travelled eastward to Russia and other Eastern European countries for creative purposes.

Communist Russia entered the narrow gate of the 'Cold War.' The novels of Alexander Solteznitsyn's were smuggled to the West to be translate in the European languages, and eventually smuggled back to Russia.

Modern Saussurean Linguistics had its own new impact on translation, with its many schools, structuralists, functionalists etc. symbolism approach was used heavily in the translation theories of people like Ezra Pound (...) in Eastern Europe, the linguists of the Prague school have had an immense impact on translation theory and poetics (cf. Jakobson) besides their purely linguistic theorizing.

22. PHONETICS

HISTORY OF PHONETIC TRANSCRIPTION

Phonetics studies the anatomy of the vocal tract, the air steams and ultimately, aims at giving an adequate representation viz. transcription of the speech sounds. While England is well known for its famous phoneticians such as Henry Sweet and Daniel Jones, the Americans seem to be lagging behind. Paradoxically it is politician and statesman Benjamin Franklin, who is mentioned in reference to spelling reforms. Phonetic studies have also a long history and numerous motivations: religion, education, politics, and pure language science.

Phonetic transcription is defined as 'a special system to record speech sounds.' It is different from the usual alphabets. The urge for this science was mainly felt by spelling reformists. They were indeed behind much advances in this field. English William Caxton's work (1422-1491) is a good example for spelling reform and printing systems. In English the difference between the spelling and the pronunciation is striking e.g. the minimal pair: *meet* vs. *meat*.

Besides spelling reformists, the urgent need for devising a phonetic transcription was also felt by travellers to exotic lands, especially missionaries, colonial administrators, travellers, historians and journalists. They all faced the problem of deciphering and hence transcribing (alien) languages. These were usually unwritten e.g. American Indian languages, or ancient languages such as Sumerian or Egyptian hieroglyphics.

The translators of the Bible, especially the Summer Institute Linguists in America, needed to transcribe unwritten languages for the translation of the Bible. Others sought the education of the 'savages,' to put it in Malinowski's terms. (See the film 'Mission').

For the linguist, the phoneticians in particular, it is a purely scientific work. He must find an unambiguous notation, which should be based on a one-to-one, segmentation of speech. The Acoustic continuum needs the proper classification and symbolic representation of its items (phonemes); one symbol for one speech sound. This is, in fact, the primary requirement for the analysis of a given language. Usually, it is based first on the identification of the binary syllable structure: consonant and vowel. It is a necessary condition before you can deal with any word formation or syntactic considerations.

As a matter of fact, any transcription is unable to capture all the phonetic details of a language. This led the phoneticians to draw a clear distinction between two major approaches to phonetic transcription: narrow and broad. These are defined as follows: "phonetic transcriptions which are relatively detailed are called **narrow transcriptions**; those which are less detailed are called **broad transcriptions**. In the broadest possible transcription, only those phonetic SEGMENTS would be noted which correspond to the functionally important units in the language." (Crystal 1980)

The transcription may begin by the impressionistic approach; i.e. transcribe the sound as you hear it. Then one of the two options is favoured according to the goals of the linguistic analysis. Narrow transcription will try and deal with consonants, vowels, but also suprasegmentals and sound features such as voice, pitch, allophones, etc. This is before you could move to the upper segments of language, such as morphemes and phrases, etc.

The phonetic Notation should:

A) Avoid ambiguity (one-to-one),

B) Use simple (beautiful) symbols,

C) Give 'key-words' as examples(!)

D) Be Ideally Universal (IPA)

"In America spelling reform led the famous American statesman, scientist and philosopher, Benjamin Franklin (1706-90) to put forward a new alphabet in 1768. It was limited to 26 symbols, of which 6 were, newly invented to take the place of the 'ambiguous letters <c j q w x y>." ((J.A. Kemp 1995)

In England, the most famous phoneticians were Alexander Melville Bell (1819-1905), Henry Sweet (1845-1912) and Daniel Jones (1881-1967). "Henry

Sweet is, perhaps the greatest of nineteenth century phoneticians, who studied under Bell." "In the nineteenth century the most prominent spelling reformer was Sir Isaac Pitman (1813-97). He was himself of comparatively humble origins, and determined from his early years to further social reform and improve the educational system by developing new alphabets to make spelling easier. He first of all developed a system of short hand (now world famous), which he called *Phonography* (published in 1837), exploring the way in which notation systems can be made to act efficiently in conveying language. Unlike earlier systems, it was based on the English sound system." (ibid)

THE IPA

The notorious IPA system or association (1897) was first led by a group of English teachers. It was based on Pitman's alphabet (v. Esperanto!!!) and on Henry Sweet's broad system (1888). It had practical teaching goals; viz., making the learning of English easier by providing a system with clarity, familiarity and economy. The IPA system is optimally based on a 'one-to-one' connection between 'sign' and 'sound.' This system is devised to help in the singular identification of the speech sound, which is crucial for meaning. It is based on the Roman alphabet, and has the ultimate goal of being generalized to international use [e.g. Arabic ^{c}ayn, French /ɔ/□]. The diacritics are avoided as much as possible. The expansion of this system tires to capture different types of nasal sounds, with 'nuances' found in different languages: palatal, velar, uvular, retroflex in English, French, etc.

[Notice Mister Pichou's "élastique" v. "couatchou" dichotomy to describe English spelling and pronunciation]

CONCLUSION

Language can be metaphorically, compared to a *coin* with two faces i.e. "sound and sense." This is to put it in the most simplistic way. Different specialists from different horizons have given their ideas about its NATURE, ORIGIN and USE. Their definitions remain dualist though: 'qawl/kalam' (Ibn Jinni), 'langue/parole' (Saussure), 'Deep/surface' (Chomsky), 'Classical/colloquial' (Ferguson) etc. 'Language' remains a puzzle to the best and a miracle for some (Einstein (?). Many were brought to the 'Labor' including philosophers (Spinoza), historians (Ibn Khaldun), psychologists (Watson), sociologists (Durkheim), and even brilliant amateurs (Jonathan Miller).

Linguistics is usually defined as the 'science of language, in the generic sense.' Its 'champions' are Swiss Saussure and American Noam Chomsky. Both were dualists. Chomsky is well known for his 'deep and surface' structures, and lately with his 'Phonetic Form and Logical Form.' Saussure is famous for his dichotomies 'langue-parole', 'signifié-signifiant'. This was the 'fashion.'

The 'fashion' was to ignore remote geographical origins of linguistics, the subject supposedly started in the twentieth century. By opposition to this narrow (ideological) denial, some suggested recognizing and benefiting from broader horizons. "The best known example is probably Leonard Bloomfield who stated in a number of his publications that he was making use of concepts and techniques that were to be found in Panini's work on Sanskrit produced some two and a half millennia ago." (...) Bloomfield described Panini's work, on other occasions, as a "monument of intelligence."

To broaden the scope of linguitics beyond Europe and North America, this book suggests a long journey in time and space, from the Far East to the Far West, covering Japan, China, India, Ancient Greece, the Arab and Jewish world and Europe of the Middle Ages.

In the FAR-EAST, we considered Japan, China, India and Babylon. The foreign influences were heavily felt in **Japan** until the coming of *Ayuisho*, which is considered as a work free from earlier Chinese and western influence. In neighboring China, some scholars consider The **Chinese** language as having the longest unbroken recorded history, and a language rather difficult to analyse from European perspectives. In India, PANINI, stands as the towering figure. His work had a great deal of influence on the scholarship in India and abroad, even nowadays. He wrote his 8 books, to set the 3.959 rules of Sanskrit morphology. His grammar is highly recognized even by modern linguists such as Bloomfield and Chomsky, two millennium later. In the Middle East, ancient Babylon can be proud of having the 1st grammatical tradition ever. Its literary Texts are dated more than 2000 years before Christ. It consists of cuneiforms diagrams. Their *Scribal School* had a primary role, in trying to put the 'world into words', as Patrick Griffiths would put it. Babylonian script remains the birth of all world alphabets.

The ancient **Greeks** and **Romans** fought each other, for hegemony for centuries. Then something strange happened: the victor and the defeated became one. The linguistic contributions were led by both sides. Romans such as DONATUS (4th AD) contributed with his *Ars Minor* and *Ars Major* grammars. ARISTOTLE was by far the greatest Greek thinker. His major was certainly logic. It led him on the path to LANGUAGE (*The Organon*).

In the **Arab** world, Persian SIBAWAIHI'S *al-Kitab* is the first grammar of Arabic. It was devised to describe the language of the Holy Qur'an. He was followed by genius Roman born IBN JINNI, the pioneer of 'generativism.' The **Hebrew** linguistic tradition lived its Golden Era in the Andalusia of the 8th to 10th c. The *Midrash* (Hebrew schools or studies) flourished. Its linguists copied "whole sale and retail from Arabic studies." (David Téné, 1995) Jewish philosophers, such as BARUCH SPINOZA, had also their contributions to logic and language. The latter's rational studies caused much annoyment among the orthodox, to the extent that they considered his works as "forged in hell by a renegade Jew and the devil."

In 19th c. Europe Historical linguistics was the fashion. It was is a '**German** affair.' It provided famous philologists such as Paul, Schleicher and the GRIMM BROTHERS. The latter were famous for their tales, and even more so for the 'Great Vowel Shift' of Indo-European languages.

The twentieth century reaction to Darwinian historicism came at the hands of the 'father of structuralism' i.e. SAUSSURE. He stressed the need for the scientific study of language; to study the system rather than the history of linguistic phenomena. The basic elements of language can only be studied in relation to their functions rather than in relation to their causes.

From structuralism, Europe moved to functionalism at the hands of PRAGUE and LONDON linguists. The functionalists of **Prague**, looked at the 'use' of language in addition to its 'shape' and 'structure'. While Saussure looked at language as a system, Prague added other dimensions i.e. the social, and the poetic functions.

England is well known for its famous phoneticians such as HENRY SWEET and DANIEL JONES. In the 16th century, The English needed spelling reforms as they were trying to make their National Language out of the multitude of unintelligible dialects they had at that time. This task required a very serious work in phonetics. Later, came ROBERT LE PAGE, who was known for his "ACTS of IDENTITY" and "FOUR RIDERS."

Because of the 'Indian genocide', the **American** sociologists, anthropologists, and descriptive linguists fet the need to record the American Indian languages before their extinction. This movement was led by brilliant scholars such Baos, Sapir and above them all BLOOMFIELD. Their 'descovery procedures' were motivated by the lack of similarity between the native American languages and any European language. Their target was the identification of the smallest unit of language viz. The « PHONEME ». Later on, Chomsky focused on syntax, LABOV on social facts, and PIKE on Bible translation.

The student of linguistics soon finds *options* and ramifications that he has to favour one at the expense of the others. The major roads of the split are: micro-linguistics (phonetics, phonology, morphology, syntax, semantics, and pragmatics.) and macro-linguistics (sociolinguistics, psycholinguistics, computational linguistics, mathematical linguistics, historical linguistics, etc.)

The problem with the appreciation of language is that of "psychic distance." The psychologist, WOLFGANG KOHLER, once remarked that it is necessary to develop a kind of *"psychic distance"* [...] from the acts that you perform naturally. You have to be able to look at them as it were from the outside, to recognize how amazing they are, before you can begin to try to find out what are the capacities on which these acts are based."(...)

ALBERT EINSTEIN once said, " There are two ways to live your life. One is as though nothing is a miracle. **The other is as though everything is a miracle**." (...) Man was given the secret and the power to give symbols to referents, i.e. different places, people, and objects by naming them. "Language" is indeed a **miracle**. This can be clearly seen when we try to imagine a world without *Language*.

GLOSSARY

ACCENT

The prominence of syllable in terms of stress.

AFFIX

Element added to the base of a word e.g. *en-joy-able*.

ALGORITHM

A computer science term meaning referring to a program.

ANALOGY

Mental similarities established between two or more elements. The structuring/building of new words based on previous patterns, *wazn/qiyas* in Arabic grammar and Logic.

ANAPHORIC

A reference shared by two or more noun phrases as in: *I don't like [Harry]$_1$ because [the fool]$_1$ hates linguistics.*

APHASIA

The loss of the ability to understand or produce speech because of brain damage. In 1860, French doctor Paul Broca contributed an amazing advance to neurological science by discovering brain lateralization and speech pathology. He discovered that the lower front lobe of the left hemisphere was responsible for the production of speech. In 1874, Austrian Wernicke reported nine cases of patients that reflected Broca's aphasia. They were fluent speakers but only uttered incoherent nonsense. Wernicke's patients did not comprehend the difference between 'come' and 'go'.

ARISTOTLE (384-322 BC)

"Aristotle built his fame on several disciplines but mostly on logos (logic/language?). For him logic and language go hand-in-hand. In his famous book *The Organon*, he set notions such as the 10 categories, propositions and contradiction."

BEHAVIOURISM

Behaviourism is attributed to B. Watson's introspection psychology, which analyses human behaviour. It is obvious that all languages were spoken before the written words took over. So, language is essentially a human behaviour. Writing is not language; it is simply a way of recording language by means of visible marks. In order to show the usage of language, Leonard Bloomfield takes into consideration two major things: stimulus and response. Language, according to Bloomfield, can be explained in behaviouristic terms. He explained this concept of his by giving the story of Jack and Jill as an example: "Jack and Jill are walking down a lane. Jill is hungry. She sees an apple in a tree. She makes a noise with her larynx, tongue and lips. Jack vaults the fence, climbs the tree, takes the apple, brings it to Jill, and places it in her hand. Jill eats the apple." (Bloomfield 1933)

BINDING

Chomskian reference rules (cf. Lectures on Government and Binding 1981).

CASE GRAMMAR

A grammatical category used in the analysis of word classes. Different forms (endings) of a word depending on its function in the sentence.

CICERO (-43 BC)

Roman writer, politician and orator.

COGNITIVE

Having to do with knowledge, e.g. cognitive meaning is that part of meaning of words and sentences judged as 'stylistically' neutral. Words can be cognitively synonymous, but may different in their connotations e.g. *popular* v. *common*.

DERIVATION

The morphological process of adding affixes to the stem, e.g. good-*ness*!

DIALECT

A special variety of a language relative to a region. Communication can easily break among speakers of different dialects of the same language. Bloomfield reports that a London cabman did not understand him, when he asked to be driven to the *comedy theatre*. Bloomfield had forgotten himself and spoken the American form of the first vowel in *comedy*, and this Englishman could take it only as a representative of the vowel phoneme in a word like *car*, so that Bloomfield was really asking for a *carmody theatre*, which does not exist.

DIGLOSSIA

Diglossia has to do with two co-existing forms of the same language as found in Arabic viz. classical Arabic and different dialects; Egyptian, Syrian, north

African, etc. one being the prestige form used in mosques, mass media and the other in markets and amongst family and friends, according to the social situation or the needs of the moment. (Ferguson, 1959)

DISCOVERY ROCEDURES

A set of techniques that mechanically apply to data to give the correct grammatical analysis of a language, according to the Bloomfieldian school.

DISTINCTIVE FEATURES

A feature which crucial for the distinction between two elements such as voice in bit v. pit (See, *The Sound Pattern of English,* Chomsky and Halle 1968).

DISTRIBUTIONALISM

Position of an item in a structure (paradigms and syntagms).

EMPIRICAL

Having to do with experience rather than theory.

ENTAILMENT

The entailments of a proposition are its logical consequences, e.g. *John was killed* entails *John is dead*.

EPISTEMOLOGY

The part of philosophy that deals with the way we know things.

GENERATIVE

A mathematic grammar defining a finite set of rules to yield an infinite set of sentences.

GOVERNMENT

Relationship between words within a sentence. Each word is affected by another in its word ending and grammatical function, in Arabic *kitab* can end with – *un, -an, -in* depending on its governor viz. initial position, verb or preposition.

HEURISTIC DEVICE

A method for solving problems, which is based on practical ways as relying on previous experience and analogy.

HUMBOLDT (1767-1835)

German linguist and anthropologist, founder of Berlin University (1809).

IDEOGRAMS

A sign or symbol, used in the writing system of China; a direct representation of the referent (thing).

IDIOLECT

The individual's proper language.

JAKOBSON ROMAN (1896-1982)

Roman Jacobson was a Russian born American linguist and Slavic-language scholar, a principle founder of the European movement in structural linguistics known as the Prague school. The European political situation of the 30', compelled him to flee successively to the University of Copenhagen, Oslo, Uppsala (Sweden) where he served as visiting professor. In 1941 he reached New York City, where he taught at Columbia University (1943-9). He was professor of Slavic languages, literature and general linguistics at Harvard University (1949-67). Among his important contributions are the notions of "distinctive features" and "poetics."

LANGUAGE CHANGE

Language changes over time in pronunciation and meaning, e.g. the (US) word 'geek,' used to mean 'ugly.' A few decades later it means 'socially inept.'

MARTINET ANDRÉ (1908-1999)

André Martinet was an imminent French linguist working at Paris III. His major book is , *L'economie des changements phonétiques* (1955). For him; language is in a state of unstable balance between "communication" and "least effort." It is a structure endowed with an organic unity and a system of feedback. People tend to go naturally for an economy of efforts in language as in other fields of life too. But this represents a danger for communication itself, which may break at certain points. So, the language structure has to accommodate for these two conflicting needs: the least effort and communication. This dialectics leads language to an ever-lasting process of change. Still, according to Martinet, only those changes of big functional effect tend to persist.

MENTALISM

Having to do with the innate capacities of the mind as opposed to behaviourism (experience earned from outside world).

MOOD

A grammatical category affecting verbs, indicating, whether it is indicative, subjunctive, imperative, etc.

MORPHEME

Smallest unit of grammar and meaning.

NEUROLINGUISTICS

Neurolinguistics has to do with language and the nervous system. "Lenneberg has reported a wealth of biological data relevant to language. These range from studies of the peripheral anatomy of the speech organs to the correlations between symptoms of language dissolution and injury to particular brain areas; from the genetic substance of certain inherited language disorders to the physiological correlates of vocalization, and from the functional organization of the central nervous system to the structural, chemical and electro-physiological changes which define the maturation of brain during the period of the first-language acquisition. But in spite of the vast accumulation of knowledge, scholars are still unable to propose a biological theory of language – a formal model of a brain mechanism consistent with the physiology described by Lenneberg and the type of psychological data summarized in the chapters by Campbell and Wales (…) and Johnson – Laird (…). Advances in knowledge have only shown even wider areas of **ignorance**." (Lyons 1970)

PAVLOV (1849-1936)

Ivan Petrovich Pavlov was a Russian physician and physiologist, winner of the Nobel Prize, famous for his experiments on dogs, considered as the father of psychological BEHAVIORISM.

PF

Phonetic Form v. Logical Form.

PHONEME

The smallest (phonetic) unit of language.

PHRASE STRUCTURE RULES

A generative (mathematical) grammar suggested by Chomsky (1957) capable of generating an infinite number of sentences from a finite number of rules as:

S →NP+VP

VP→ V+NP

NP→DET+N

The boy hit the ball, the ball hit the boy, a ball hit a boy, etc., etc.

PORT ROYAL (16th c.)

Originally, Portroyal was a famous Cistercian Covent in the valley de Chévreuse southwest of Paris that launched a number of culturally important institutions. The Arnauld family became its patrons. Antoine Arnold's book *Grammaire logique et générale*, is probably the most outstanding linguistic work of Port Royal tradition.

PRAGMATICS

Pragmatics deals with utterances, by which we mean specific events, the intentional acts of speakers at times and places, typically involving language.

PROPOSITION

Logical term for a declarative sentence v. performative.

PSYCHOLINGUISTICS

A branch of linguistics which establishes the connection between linguistic behaviour and psychological processes such as memory, learning, perception, attention, etc.

RATIONAL

Having to do with reason, logic.

ROOT

In morphology, the part of the word that remains after all morphological transformations have been removed.

SEMANTICS

The study of language meaning, especially the meaning of words and sentences. It is further divided into 'sense' and 'reference.'

SEMIOLOGY (OR SEMIOTICS)

A science of signs within a community.

SHAW'S (PYGMALION)

Bernard Shaw is an Irish famous playwright (1856-1950). Most of his plays criticize society in a humoristic way. He thinks that social classes can easily be noticed through the language people use. The language of the high class is different from that of the lower class. In his play "Pygmalion", a cultured man from the high-class took the challenge to make a good mannered sophisticated lady, from a lower class young girl. He took her as an experiment, taught her how to speak and behave like a woman from the high class. She, indeed, benefited from his efforts and eventually was taken for a 'princess' in a high class party. Nobody could realize that she was in fact from the lower class. (Mom)

SKINNER (1904- 1990)

Burrhus Frederic skinner, American psychologist. Influential thinker of behaviourist school.(*Verbal Behaviour*)

STRUCTURALISM

A system in which each element depends on the others.

SUPRASEGMENTAL

Suprasegmental features are superimposed on the segments (vowels and consonants) such as stress, intonation, length.

SUTRAS

A Hinduism/Buddhist brief composition Way of the Elders, and Greater Vehicle.

SYLLABLE

A unit of pronunciation larger than the phoneme and smaller than the word e.g. *ne-ver-the-less*, contains 4 syllables. A syllable consists necessarily of a vowel and a number of consonants varying from one zero to 4 (5?) the vowel with one syllable is called monosyllabic e.g. *it*, polysyllabic with two or more. (see Ben Rochd *Generative Grammar*, ms, University of Washington).

SYNTAX

A branch of linguistics that studies the combination of words into sentences.

TRANSFORMATION

A (syntactic rule) that operates under specific conditions, by giving a structural description then moves to a structural change, as in: *the boy hit the ball* → *the ball was hit by the boy*.

UMLAUT

A relationship between front and back vowels found in German, and represented by two dots over the basic vowel. Historically, a change that happened in old German, realized by the fronting of certain vowels.

VOICE

The vibrations of the vocal cords as in *bit v. pit*.

WATSON (1878-1958)

John Broadus Watson is an American psychologist pioneer of behaviourism.

ZERO

Zero morpheme refers to certain affixes like the plural of fish-Ø v. table-s.

BIBLIOGRAPHY

Abdu-Ghany, A. 1981. Government-Binding in Classical Arabic. PhD, University of Texas at Austin.

Alexander, L.G. 1972. Sixty Steps to Précis. Longman. London.

Allen JPB. and Paul Van Buren. 1975. Chomsky: Selected Readings. OUP, Oxford.

Al Nasir,A. 1985. Sibawaihi, the Phonologist. PhD, York University.

Al Seghayar,M. .1988. On the Syntax of Small Clauses in Arabic. MA, Ottawa University.

Al Waer, M .1980. An Interview with American Linguist Noam Chomsky', Dept. of Linguistics and Philosophy. MIT.

Allwood, J.1987. Logic . CUP, Cambridge.

Aitchinson, J. *Language Change: Progress or Decay*, University Books, NY 1985.

Baalbaki R. 2004. Grammarians and Grammatical Theory in the Medieval Arabic Tradition. Padstow. Cornwall.

Bellout, Z.1987. Moroccan Arabic syllabic structure. DES university of Casablanca.

Ben Rochd, E.1979. French Passive. MA, York University.

Ben Rochd, E.1979. Generalized Binding and Pronominalization in Classical Arabic. PhD, The National University of Ireland.

Ben Rochd, E.1979. Barriers and Arabic. Linguistica Communicatio 3, 1.

Ben Rochd, E.1979. "Aoun's Generalized Binding and the Arabic Evidence." Revue Faculté des Lettrers, Oujda.

Ben Rochd, E. 1979. Traditional Linguistics. Bawariq, Oujda.

Ben Rochd, E.1982. American Linguistics. Najah, Casablanca.

Ben Rochd, E. 1994. Generative Grammar. Ms. University of Washington.

Ben Rochd, E . 2019. Tradition in Linguistics. Bod. Paris.

Ben Rochd, E. 2020a. Evolution of Chomsky's Transformational Grammar. Bod. Paris.

Ben Rochd, E. 2020 b. Words. Bod. Paris.

Ben Rochd, E. 2021a. Sibawaihi's Transformational Grammar. Bod. Paris.

Ben Rochd, E. 2021b. Die Worter. Bod. Paris.

Ben Rochd, E. 2021c. Schools of Linguitics. Bod. Paris.

Benveniste, E.1966. Problèmes de linguistique générale. Galimar, Paris.

Bittner, M. and K. Hale. 1993. "Ergativity." MIT, Cambridge.

Bloomfield, L.1933. Language. Holt, New York.

Borer, H.1983. Parametric Syntax. Foris, Dordrecht.

Borer, H.1987. "Anaphoric AGR." GLOW, Venice.

Brame, M.1970. Arabic Phonology. PhD MIT.

Busse, W.1974. Klasse Transitivitat Valenz. Fink, Munich.

Carter, M.1968. A Study of Sibawaihi's Principles of Grammatical Analysis. PhD, Oxford.

Chomsky, N.1957. Syntactic Structures. Mouton, The Hague.

Chomsky, N.1965. Aspects of the Theory of Syntax. MIT, Cambridge.

Chomsky, N.1972. Language and Mind. Harcourt, New York.

Chomsky, N.1981. Lectures on Government and Binding. Foris, Dordrecht.

Chomsky, N.1982. Some Concepts and Consequences of the Theory of Government and Binding. MIT, Cambridge.

Chomsky, N.1986. Barriers. MIT, Cambridge.

Chomsky, N.1988. Language and Problems of Knowledge. MIT, Cambridge.

Chomsky, N.1997. Minimalist Program. MIT, Cambridge.

Chomsky, N. and M. Halle. 1968. The Sound Pattern of English. Harper and Row, New York.

Comrie, B. 1991 'On the Importance of Arabic to General Linguistic Theory', in Bernard Comrie and Mushira eid (eds): Perspectives on Arabic Linguistics III, Amsterdam, John Benjamins

Crystal, D.1985. A Dictionary of Linguistics and Phonetics. Blackwell, Oxford.

Descartes, R.1637. Discours de la méthode. Les Classiques du Peuple, Paris.

Drimmer, 1968. Black History. Doubleday and CIE. NY.

Emonds, J.1987. "Parts of Speech in Generative Grammar." Linguistic analysis 17, 1-42.

Fassi-Fehri, A.1982. Lisaniyat wa LuRa 'arabiya. 'uwidat, baris.

Fassi-Fehri, A.1990. "Agreement, Incorporation, Pleonastics, and VSO-SVO order." MIT, Cambridge.

Ferguson, CA. 1959.' Diglossia.' word 15.325-40.

Fromkin, V. and R. Rodman. 1983. An Introduction to Language. Holt-Sanders, New York.

Gleason, H.1969. An Introduction to Descriptive Linguistics. Holt-Sanders, New York.

Guamgami, M. 2002, *A Philosophical Approach to English*, ms, Oujda.

Haegeman, L.1991. Government and Binding Theory. Blackwell, Oxford.

Hale, K.1983. Walpiri and the Grammar of Non-Configurational Languages." Natural language. NLLT 1, 5-47.

Hoeksema, J.1987. "Logic of Natural Language." Linguistic analysis 11, 155-184.

Jackendoff, R. 1990. Semantic structures. MIT. Cambridge, Mass.

Jones, D. 1997. Everyman's Pronouncing Dictionary. Datton. NY.

Kayne, R.1975. French Syntax, the Transformational Cycle. MIT, Cambridge.

Kayne, R.1987. "Null Subjects and Clitic Climbing." GLOW, Venice.

King James Version of the Bible.

Koerner, E.F. and R.E. Asher 1995. Concise History of Language Sciences. Pergamon. Cambridge.

Le Page, R. 1980. *Acts of Identity*. ms. York University.

Lyons, J. 1970. New Horizons in Linguistics. Penguin. Middlesex.

Madkour, I.1969. L'Organon dans le monde arabe. J. Vrin, Paris.

May, R.1985. Logical Form. MIT, Cambridge.

McCarthy, J.1979. Formal Problems in Semitic Phonology and Morphology. PhD, MIT.

McCarthy, J.1990. Prosodic Morphology and Templatic Morphology. MIT, Cambridge.

Newmeyer, F. 1980. Linguistic theory in America. AP. NY.

Palmer, F.1990. Semantics. CUP, Cambridge.

Partee, B.1975. "Montague grammar." Linguistic inquiry 6, 203-300.

Pickthall M.M. The Meaning of the Glorious Koran. Mentor. NY.

Radford, A.1981. Transformational Syntax. CUP, Cambridge.

Radford, A.1988. Transformational Grammar. CUP, Cambridge.

Riemsdijk, H and E. Williams. 1986. Theory of Grammar. MIT, Cambridge.

Rizzi, L.1982. Issues in Italian Syntax. Foris, Dordrecht.

Robins, R.H.1967. A Short History of Linguistics. CUP. Cambridge. Sampson, G. 1980 Schools of Linguistics. Hutchinson. London.

Saussure, F.1977. Course in General Linguistics. Fontana, Oxford.

Schane, S.1973. Generative Phonology. Prentice Hall, New Jersey.

Selkirk, O.1984. Phonology and Syntax. MIT, Cambridge.

Sells, P.1985. Lectures on Contemporary Syntactic Theories. CSLI, Sanford.

Sibawaihi, 1966. al-Kitab. Alam al-kitab. Beirut.

Solzhenitsyn a 1974. The Gulag Archipelago. Fontana. Suffolk.

Souaieh, I.1980. Aspects of Arabic Relative Clauses. PhD, Indiana University.

Stowell, T.1989. "Subjects, Specifiers and X-bar Theory." In Alternative Conceptions of Phrase Structure. UCP, Chicago.

Wasow, T.1975. "Anaphoric Pronouns and Bound Variables." Language 51, 368-373.

Wittgenstein, I.1958. Philosophical Investigations. Blackwell, Oxford.

Wright, W.1979. A Grammar of the Arabic Language. CUP, Cambridge.

Das weiß nur Gott!
El Mouatamid Ben Rochd

History of Linguistics

© 2021, EL MOUATAMID BEN ROCHD
Edition: BoD - Books on Demand, 12/14 rond-point des Champs-Élysées, 75008 Paris
Printing: BoD - Books on Demand, Norderstedt, Germany
ISBN: 9782322404827
Legal deposit: December 2021